With Glad and Generous Hearts

With Glad and and Generous Hearts

A PERSONAL LOOK AT SUNDAY WORSHIP

William H. Willimon

Educational Guide
by John Westerhoff III

THE UPPER ROOM
Nashville, Tennessee

WITH GLAD AND GENEROUS HEARTS

Scripture quotations not otherwise identified are from the Revised Standard Version of the Bible, copyrighted 1946, 1952, and © 1971 by the Division of Christian Education, National Council of Churches of Christ in the United States of America, and are used by permission.

Scripture quotations designated AP are the author's paraphrase.

The prayer from WE GATHER TOGETHER, p. 6, is copyright © 1980 by The United Methodist Publishing House. Used by permission.

The litany from *The Sacrament of the Lord's Supper, An Alternate Text, 1972* is copyright © 1972 by The Methodist Publishing House. Used by permission.

Illustrations by BRUCE SAYRE

Book design: John Robinson
Cover transparency: Peyton Hoge/CORN'S PHOTO SERVICE
First printing: May, 1986 (7)
Second printing: April, 1987 (7)
Library of Congress Catalog Card Number: 85-052012

ISBN 0-8358-0536-0

PRINTED IN THE UNITED STATES OF AMERICA

To
Peggy Hursey
Twenty years directing a church choir and still glad and generous.

Contents

Preface

I look upon this book as the last of a trilogy which I began with *Remember Who You Are* and *Sunday Dinner.* Many seemed to find those books helpful so now I offer this one. Whereas those books each focused on one of the sacraments, here I present a larger view of the Sunday service as a whole.

Like the earlier books, *With Glad and Generous Hearts* is written primarily for interested laypersons who wish to deepen their understanding and experience of Sunday worship. What you will read is not a technical history or theology of worship—I have done that elsewhere. This is a reflective, devotional work which should make a difference in what happens to you on Sunday morning.

My thanks to those whom I lead in worship each Sunday here in Duke Chapel, this magnificent place of prayer and praise. They often help me to worship, even when I don't feel like it. Thanks to my colleague, John Westerhoff, for again enriching one of my books with his educational introduction and learning activities. If you are using this book as a means of personal growth or with an adult class or learning group, you will be grateful for John's work.

Once again, my talented friend, Bruce Sayre, offers fine illustration, giving us glimpses of people at worship.

Thanks also to the many brothers and sisters who, in dozens of places around the world, have responded to these thoughts while they were in process. Every time I venture forth to lead a workshop, or to give a lecture or sermon, I always return home with more than I set out with. Much of the really good material in this book came as gifts from others. I hope that the same thing has happened to you so often on Sunday morning at worship that you will forgive me for making these gifts my own and offering them now to you.

WILLIAM H. WILLIMON
Duke University Chapel
Durham, North Carolina

All who believed were together and had all things
in common; and they sold their possessions
and goods and distributed them to all, as any had
need. And day by day, attending the temple
together and breaking bread in their homes, they
partook of food with glad and generous hearts,
praising God and having favor with all the people.
And the Lord added to their number day by day
those who were being saved.   —*Acts 2:44-47*

the first day of the Jewish work week, they gathered with their Christian brothers and sisters at church, probably in the evening as soon as they got off work. Eventually, relations between the Jews in the synagogue and those who were now Christians became strained. Jewish Christians were evicted from the synagogues, and Christianity, which had originally been a sectarian movement within Judaism, became a distinct religion.

For Christians, the Lord's Day, Sunday, represented the decisive new quality of their faith in Jesus. New wineskins were required for the bubbling new wine. Rather than continuing the sabbath as a day of re-creation and worship, Sunday would be the day for Christians—the day of resurrection, the first day of creation.

As recorded in *Liturgies of the Western Church*, Justin Martyr, an early Christian who eventually paid for his faith with his blood, gives us our earliest complete description (*ca.* 150 A.D.) of Sunday worship:

> On the day which is called Sunday, all who live in the cities or in the countryside gather together in one place. And the memoirs of the apostles or the writings of the prophets are read as long as there is time. Then, when the reader has finished, the president, in a discourse, admonishes and invites the people to practice these examples of virtue. Then we all stand up together and offer prayers. And, as we mentioned before, when we have finished the prayer, bread is presented, and wine with water; the president likewise offers up prayers and thanksgivings according to his ability, and the people assent by saying, Amen. The elements which have been "eucharistized" are distributed and received by each one; and they are sent to the absent by the deacons.

Those who are prosperous, if they wish, contribute what each one deems appropriate; and the collection is deposited with the president; and he takes care of the orphans and the widows, and those who are needy because of sickness or other cause, and the captives, and the strangers who sojourn amongst us—in brief, he is the curate of all who are in need.

Justin describes a people who "gather together in one place," read their sacred writings, interpret them, sing, pray, offer their gifts, say a blessing, eat together, then scatter into the world. You are familiar with this pattern of worship. Two thousand years later, you are still enacting this phenomenon at your church on Sunday morning.

This dynamic of gathering, hearing, acting, and scattering in Jesus' name is at the heart of Christian worship, the very center of the Good News. So let us begin with a definition of who you are as a Christian: *A Christian is someone who has heard the call of Jesus to "follow me." In obedience to Jesus' invitation, Christians now gather with others who have heard the same invitation in order to listen to Jesus, to speak to him, to eat and drink in his presence, and to celebrate his work in the world. Then we scatter. Having been refreshed and re-created on Sunday, we are now able to live as his disciples in ways that show forth the Good News to others. We are Sunday people.*

You rise from your Sunday morning reverie and begin to prepare to go to church. Worship has already begun for you, the moment you opened your eyes and greeted the new day, the moment you felt gratitude for being alive. Now you will intensify and claim that experience in worship by gathering with others who share with you a glad desire to respond to a God who has reached out gladly to you in something so simple, so holy, as morning sunlight on a patio.

You put on your best clothes. You think of whom you may see at church, what the sermon will be about, which anthem the choir will sing, who has baked the bread for Communion. You leave home expectantly, refreshed, pleased to be part of the gathering in Jesus' name.

Thus you have recapitulated in your own life on this Sunday the dying and rising, the re-creation and resurrection, which is at the heart of the Christian life. It is as if you have been reborn, resurrected, made over for this new day. Sunday is happening to you, even as it happens to the church.

In this book we shall explore together the implications of what it means for us to be part of this people who gather on Sunday. We shall do this by taking various aspects of a typical Sunday morning service and focusing upon each of these acts of worship as a picture of what it means to be a Christian in today's world. It is my hope that you will see new meaning within your own experience of corporate worship and that your own spiritual life will be enriched.

1.

Gathering

Lift up your hearts.

My soul thirsts for God,
  for the living God.
When shall I come and behold
  the face of God?

—Psalm 42:2

You drive through sleepy, Sunday neighborhoods, down the freeway, taking the exit that leads you to your church. The streets are relatively empty this morning. Perhaps there was a time when Sunday traffic caused as much congestion as the Monday morning rush hour. If that were ever true, it is no longer.

As one who is going to church, you are obviously in a minority. How do you feel about that? What makes you different from your next-door neighbors who view Sunday as simply a free day for trips to the beach? Why does church mean so much to you and so little to them?

Faith as Focus

Faith is a gift, Paul says, a mystery. Some receive and respond to faith, some don't. Is it so surprising that Christians should be a minority? The church has thrived under such circumstances. Perhaps in your lifetime the American church shall return to its minority status. You wonder to yourself: If Christianity is true, why doesn't everyone see things as I do? Why aren't the roads filled with people coming to church?

The problem may be one of focus. In the modern world, many have things out of focus. Have you ever looked through the lens of a telescope? At first, all you see is a blur. A telescope is effective to the degree that the user is able to bring things in focus. Carefully, patiently, you must adjust the lens until the planets come into view. Then, as if by magic, what appeared to be only a blur of light becomes the planet Mars—red, patterned, intricate, and beautiful.

Many modern people appear to have life out of focus. Novelist Walker Percy comments in his book *Lost in the Cosmos*, "How can you survive in the Cosmos, about which you know more and more while knowing less and less about yourself, this despite ten thousand self-help books, one hundred psychotherapists, and one hundred million fundamentalist Christians?"

Percy's title, *Lost in the Cosmos: The Last Self-help Book*, says it all: We are more adept at scientifically penetrating the universe and less competent in understanding ourselves. We send space craft into the heavens, moving farther away from our world, as if we have despaired of ever being at home on our planet. Science and technology have brought us many wonders but have, in the process, retarded our ability to wonder. We know everything about the planet Mars except that it is beautiful. Lost in the cosmos, we wander as exiles, aliens in our own land, drifting, cut loose from old moorings, traveling from a place we have long ago forgotten, being carried along to we know not where.

Before coming to church this morning, you glanced at the headlines in the Sunday paper. Did those headlines suggest that humanity is making progress?

As you drive along the freeway, the radio is blaring in your ear, telling you to buy this, to check out that. With steady, relentless, rhythmic beat it tells you how to be happy, have a good time, make friends, look young forever—all for only $9.95, this week, while supplies last. With Walkman portable radios and Musak continuous background, no wonder we suffer from auditory overload, noise, chatter, hucksterism, everyone speaking, no one listening, a throbbing, deafening beat which masks the frightening silence of contemporary culture.

What is happening to your ears is also being done to your eyes. Billboards line the roadside full of grinning, happy faces proclaiming the blessings to be received from their new products. These are set along great caverns of buildings, gray, drab highrise apartments, long rows of warehouses. Everything is so big and towering, yet so empty.

Is it any wonder, with all this noise and these flashing images, that people become numb, distracted, overloaded? The world bombards us with the same numbing, deafening, blinding assault as if it were all one great television screen. Our eyes glaze over. Before long, we don't hear the voices or the music anymore out of sheer self-protection and exhaustion. We withdraw into ourselves in order to maintain our sanity. If one comes along who speaks a clear, simple, honest, "Follow me," our deafness to his invitation may be tragic, but at least it is understandable. This is what the world does to people.

A major thrust of Jesus' ministry was to heal people of blindness and deafness:

> They came to Jericho; and as he was leaving Jericho with his disciples and a great multitude, Bartimaeus, a blind beggar, the son of Timaeus, was sitting by the roadside. And when he heard that it was Jesus of Nazareth, he began to cry out and say, "Jesus, Son of David, have mercy on me!" And many rebuked him, telling him to be silent; but he cried out all the more, "Son of David, have mercy on me!" And Jesus stopped and said, "Call him." And they called the blind man, saying to him, "Take heart; rise, he is calling you." And throwing off his mantle he sprang up and came to Jesus. And Jesus said to him, "What do you want me to do for you?" And the blind man said to him, "Master, let me receive my sight." And Jesus said to him, "Go your way; your faith has made you well." And immediately he received his sight and followed him on the way.
>
> —Mark 10:46-52

I take this story of the healing of Bartimaeus as a sort of parable of us on Sunday morning in our gathering. We are struck blind and deaf by the world. But at least we have heard the call of Jesus. We come in our infirmity, obeying the invitation to "take heart; rise, he is calling you." Then he touches us in the hour of worship, he listens to us and we listen to him.

Then he says, "Go your way; your faith has made you well." Then we leave church to follow him on the way.

In the Gospels, blindness and deafness are depicted as tragic disabilities. But they are not as tragic as the spiritual inability to see and hear who Jesus is. At Jesus' birth, Herod the king, thought to be so wise and powerful, is unable to know who he is. Only the Magi, aliens from afar, are able to see. The Gospel of John is full of stories of people who see but do not see and hear but do not hear.

Both blindness and deafness are terrible handicaps. In my family people begin to lose their hearing in their sixties due to a hereditary condition. Deafness is particularly tragic because it is invisible. Other people speak, we are looking at them, nodding politely in agreement, but we don't hear. What is more troubling, a person who suffers a gradual loss of hearing may be unaware that he or she is becoming deaf. They may believe the problem lies in others' inability to speak clearly rather than in their inability to hear.

The deafness and blindness occasioned by the nature of contemporary life is one way of explaining why you have seen and heard something whereas many of your neighbors (perhaps the majority of them) have not. As a Christian, you may be morally no better than they, in fact, you may feel that you are a good deal less moral than your unbelieving neighbors. The primary difference between the believer and the nonbeliever is that the believer has seen and heard something whereas the nonbeliever has not. That does not mean that you are better, or more sensitive, or intelligent—for Christians believe that faith is a gift. It means that your eyes and ears have been graciously, quite inexplicably opened to a presence and a voice which says, "Follow me."

Where Two or Three Are Gathered

You are going to church, gathering with fellow Christians to worship in order to get things in focus. Because of the incessant distraction of life in the world, from time to time you must refocus. It is so easy to become distracted, to allow the nonessentials to elbow out the essentials, to see everything except the obvious. Knowing this, you come to church on Sunday. In so doing, you are repeating an ancient pattern of gathering with those who follow Jesus.

After the cruel crucifixion of Jesus, the frightened disciples who forsook him and fled into the dark night (Matt. 26:56) could have remained scattered. But no, soon they had crept through the deserted streets and alleyways and were "all together in one place" (Acts 2:1). They gathered to reassure one another, to share their stories of what had happened to each of them during the last, terrible days, to forgive one another for their cowardice and betrayal at Golgotha, to wait together for the promised returning of their master.

You are one with these first disciples. Today you are enacting the same dynamic which Justin Martyr described nearly two thousand years ago: "On the day which is called Sunday, all who live in the cities or in the countryside gather together in one place."

In a sense, that is what the church is—a gathering together in one place of those who are disciples. The Greek word *ecclesia* is the earliest word for the church. It means, literally, both the "assembly" or "congregation," and the act of assembling. The Good News

gathers a crowd. The words and presence of Jesus attract people. As you park your car in front of your church and offer to help Mrs. Smith carry in her flowers for the altar, you are gathering for worship. From all parts of the city, from different classes and social backgrounds, different races and different needs, the people of God are gathering, church is happening, taking visible form once again. You—standing, now in the narthex, receiving a bulletin from the usher, leaning down to speak to a child, inviting a visitor to sit beside you—are part of it, now a member of the Body.

Getting It All Together

Make a joyful noise to the Lord, all the lands!
   Serve the Lord with gladness!
   Come into his presence with singing!
. . . .
Enter his gates with thanksgiving,
   and his courts with praise!
   Give thanks to him, bless his name!
                       —Psalm 100:1-2,4

O come, let us worship and bow down,
   let us kneel before the Lord, our Maker!
For he is our God,
   and we are the people of his pasture,
   and the sheep of his hand.
                       —Psalm 95:6-7

Note how many of the psalms call people to gather to worship. For all the reasons we have mentioned, people must be called to worship, gathered. Our faith requires continual refocusing, re-membering, re-collection. A major function of the church is to help us to pay attention.

As you sit in the pew awaiting the beginning of the service, you are already participating in the first act of worship. Think of this time not as pointless preliminaries, but as an important first act of worship. As the people gather, you are gathering your thoughts, beginning the essential process of settling in, centering yourself, focusing your attention.

From the random scattering of thought your mind begins to gather itself for worship: "I wonder where the Smiths have been for the past few weeks. I hope they're not ill. If they're not here today, I need to call them when I get home. Jane has her new baby with her today. The sermon title is, 'Coming Back Home.' I wonder what the preacher will do with that? Probably it will be related to the Gospel, Luke 14. What will I do this afternoon? Go to the beach? Read that new novel? Perhaps I'll need to call on the Smiths. I'll introduce the visitors beside me to our evangelism chairperson."

Don't worry that your mind jumps from one thought to another during this or any other act of worship. That's OK. Relax, let your mind sort through the images, feelings, sounds. One trouble with your Monday-through-Saturday world is that it allows you so little time for quiet, for free-association of thought. You have that much-needed space now. Enjoy it. Do not be surprised that your mind roams. Eventually it shall focus; its wandering shall eventually lead you to God.

This time of gathering has been an overlooked, neglected part of our Sunday service. Presumably

there may have been a time in some churches—
where the people all lived in the same little town,
shopped at the same stores, walked the same streets,
and saw one another all week long—when there was
little need to be intentional about gathering on Sunday. Today, in most churches, this coherent, unified
world has disappeared. Sunday is usually a gathering
of virtual strangers who have not seen one another
since last Sunday.

So time and attention must be given to gathering.
Here, in these moments before the service formally
begins, the church is re-collected, re-membered.
Even as you have been collecting your thoughts, so
God's people must be assembled. Here as people
greet one another, share what has happened to them
during the past week, welcome visitors, prepare to
worship, the body of Christ is literally being "re-
membered," the members of that body are once again
taking visible form. If we neglect this gathering, if we
just assume that it happens, it probably will not happen. The service begins without an assembly, we limp
through our worship with a disjointed body.

Probably this gathering began long before you left
for church—as you sat, deep in reflection on your
patio and contemplated going to worship. Most of us
could do a better job of gathering ourselves for worship while we are still at home. The Jewish synagogue service begins with evening prayers around
the family dinner table. We ought to consider the de-
velopment of some disciplined, personal devotional
time before leaving for church. For example, some
families forgo breakfast or at least eat light on those
Sundays when the Lord's Supper is to be celebrated
at their church. They have found that this time of

fasting is helpful preparation for Communion, a way of whetting the appetite, so to speak, for this holy meal.

In similar fashion, many find that a short period of silence immediately before the service can help improve our receptivity to the music and the words of worship. This preservice silence becomes a time to clear away the accumulated auditory bric-a-brac so that we are better able to hear.

Many congregations struggle with this issue of silence. They are directed by the bulletin to "Enter in silence and be in prayer before the service begins." But they often find this difficult to achieve. The whispering and chattering before the service continues, nevertheless. This chatter may be an important part of the act of gathering. The question is not, "Should we talk or should we keep quiet?" but the more basic "What do we need to do to gather ourselves for worship?"

A friend of mine tells the story of a young pastor who labored heroically to get his loquacious congregation to keep silence during the moments before the service began. Time and again he told them, "The noise before the service is irreverent." One Sunday, the pastor entered the sanctuary and thought it sounded like a turkey farm. He really lowered the boom on them, told them again about the need to be silent and reverent before worship.

After the service was ended, as the pastor spoke to people at the door of the church, an old farmer approached him. "Young man," he said, "I heard what you said about our talking before the service. Let me tell you what I was talking about. As I entered church, Sam told me about Joe and Mary's milk cow, how she had jumped the fence and tore her udder. Well, I knew that Joe and Mary needed that cow for milk for their kids. So I told Sam that, after church, we'd get one of my cows and take it over there to Joe and Mary's house and take their cow to the vet. Now, after I told Joe and Mary about that, I was ready to worship."

All that seemingly pointless chatter was really necessary preparation for worship. Without it, there would be no church to worship, the prayer and praise would have been premature, hypocritical.

A certain amount of preservice chatter is helpful in gathering us for worship. Somber, stilted silence gives people the impression that the congregation is cold and uncaring. Yet, as we noted earlier, silence can be helpful too.

A recent architectural directive from the Roman Catholic bishops suggests that the entrance hall or narthex leading into the sanctuary or place of worship ought to be nearly as large as the sanctuary itself, filled with comfortable, living-room-type furniture, a coffee urn and doughnuts, so worshipers will be encouraged to linger, visit, and gather before the service.

I once visited a congregation in Indiana which had its fellowship hall joined to its sanctuary with a set of glass doors. After church school, people flowed out into the fellowship hall. Refreshments were served, various church committees and groups had tables and booths set up in the room recruiting volunteers. A few minutes before eleven, the pastor mounted a table, welcomed people, introduced visitors, made announcements. When the choir began the first hymn, people joined in and then followed the pastor and choir into the sanctuary in joyous procession. Now, that's gathering!

I advise a mix between necessary greeting and talking and necessary silence and focusing. Let the congregation gather in warmth and friendly conversation. Encourage people to move about and greet one another, welcome visitors and thereby create the warm, family-like setting which fosters good worship. The organ should not be played during this time. An organ prelude is a separate act of worship and should be savored on its own, not used as background music for the congregation's chatter. At the time when worship is to begin, the pastor should step forward and welcome people, particularly the visitors. Here the pastor sets the tone for the service with warmth, enthusiasm, and a sense of expectancy. Announcements should be made here, as a means of setting our worship within the context of congregational activity. I believe that laypersons should make the announcements rather than the pastor. If the youth group is having a car wash to raise money for world hunger, the president of the group should announce it. If there has been a death in the congregation or persons are hospitalized, call this to the attention of the congregation now so members can keep these persons in mind as they move through the service.

If there are unusual or unfamiliar aspects of today's service, call those to the attention of the congregation. An unfamiliar hymn could be rehearsed at this time so that people may participate more fully when the hymn is sung later. Keep announcements and rehearsal short. Then the pastor says, "Let us worship." The prelude begins and the congregation is now in silence, gathered and ready for worship.

You have now been gathered with fellow Christians. Your wandering mind begins to focus as the organ music leads you into the service. At the end of the prelude, the pastor's voice breaks the silence from the rear of the congregation.

"Lift up your hearts."

The congregation responds with one voice, "We lift them up unto the Lord."

The congregation stands as the choir processes in, all singing, "Holy, holy, holy! Lord God Almighty! Early in the morning our song shall rise to Thee."

You raise your voice with theirs, one great procession now, moving forward, intensifying what you have heretofore only vaguely felt. Focusing, you begin to hear and see clearly what your Monday-through-Saturday world has but hinted, saying with your wandering ancestor Jacob, when heaven's ladder was lowered to his reach, "Surely the Lord is in this place; and I did not know it" (Gen. 28:16).

2.

Confession
Let us confess our sin before God and one another.

Isaiah said, "Woe is me! For I am lost; for I am a man of unclean lips, and I dwell in the midst of a people of unclean lips; for my eyes have seen the King, the Lord of hosts!"   —*Isaiah 6:5*

I n the year that King Uzziah died (742 B.C.), a young man entered the temple to pray. It was a time of social unrest and political uncertainty in Israel. Like many young people today, Isaiah was uncertain about what lay ahead for him and his society.

Then, as the priest intoned the liturgy, with clouds of incense drifting through the vast, dark spaces of the temple, Isaiah was brought to his knees by a vision: "I saw the Lord sitting upon a throne, high and lifted up; and his train filled the temple. Above him stood the seraphim; each had six wings: with two he covered his face, and with two he covered his feet, and with two he flew" (Isa. 6:1-2).

The heavens seemed to open over the ark of the covenant. Isaiah beheld the very face of God.

You have begun this Sunday's service with a hymn which was inspired by Isaiah 6:

Holy, holy, holy! Lord God Almighty!
Early in the morning our song shall rise to Thee.

As you sing, you note that, like all the hymns in the
first part of the hymnal, this one sings of the majesty
of God and the joy of gathering in God's presence. We
come before God, process toward the altar, and cry
aloud with the heavenly hosts:

Holy, holy, holy! all the saints adore Thee,
Casting down their golden crowns
     around the glassy sea;
Cherubim and Seraphim falling down before Thee,
Which wert, and art, and evermore shalt be.

What was Isaiah's response to this vision? "Woe is
me! For I am lost; for I am a man of unclean lips, and I
dwell in the midst of a people of unclean lips; for my
eyes have seen the King, the Lord of hosts!" (Isa. 6:5).

The Fear of the Lord Is the Beginning of Wisdom

To come before the holiness of God is to be reminded of our unholiness. To see the love of God is to
be judged for all the ways in which we betray that
love. The Bible declares that it is a fearful thing to fall
into the hands of the living God. A *fearful* thing. Our
worship would be an easy matter if the church were a
weekly meeting of religiously inclined dilettantes to
further the study of the deity, or a memorial dinner to
resuscitate the fading memory of a departed hero.
Worship is more risky because to worship is to risk
falling into the loving grasp of the living God.

Such love can blow us to bits, turn us inside out. So

we tiptoe around the presence, turning our sanctuaries into carpeted bedrooms, fearful that we might awaken the slumbering Presence. We chatter nervously before the music begins, the way people always do when they are scared of what may happen next. We transform our worship into the backslapping conviviality of a Kiwanis Club dinner, everyone smiling and reassuring one another that this is only church, only Sunday, nothing over which to be alarmed.

Isaiah knew better. In your better moments, *you* know better. To stand in the presence of God is to be brought to our knees. "Woe is me!" is the result of adoration. "Holy, holy, holy!" followed by "Woe is me!" is the way people behave around a burning bush or a ladder brought down from heaven. The recognition of ultimate goodness and holiness draws from the astonished heart something akin to Peter's, "Depart from me, for I am a sinful man, O Lord" (Luke 5:8).

People sometimes complain that in our attempts to foster Sunday morning warmth and friendliness we have trivialized the worship of God, made it over into the banal chant of the kindergartner:

> Good morning to you,
> Good morning to you.
> We're all in our places with
> Bright sunshine faces.
> This is the way to start a new day.

When was the last time you felt fear in worship? Do you feel just a bit uneasy even now, as if you are being led, by the procession of the choir, by the singing of this hymn, into some mysterious, unknown place of power?

Yet we speak too negatively here. The biblical "fear of the Lord" which is said to be the "beginning of wisdom" is more akin to awe and adoration than terror. When our sense of God's love is heightened, say, when we join our voices here at the beginning of the service, our defenses crumble. The masks that we work so diligently to keep in place seem less useful. We feel drawn toward a love which, though it judges us, also frees us from our self-protection and pretensions. Recoil before the face of God gives way to trust. We find that we are willing to be exposed to more truth than we thought we could endure. The God who was previously regarded as our enemy, the Judge, becomes our Friend who judges us so that we might become more true to ourselves. We find that we are willing to stand in the light of God's truth, even though it exposes our falsehood, because we are again confident that in God's light is our life.

Confession, "Woe is me . . . for I am a man of unclean lips, and I dwell in the midst of a people of unclean lips," is made possible by humility. To worship is a humbling exercise. We're not talking about some sort of self-deprecating groveling here. Much "humility" is self-conscious and phoney. You can't decide to be humble—you either are or you are not.

Rather, humility occurs as a gracious by-product of worship, a result of the self-forgetfulness which happens when we sing, "Holy, holy, holy!" We become, in the words of another favorite hymn, "lost in wonder, love, and praise" and are thereby willing to abandon our incessant need to be right.

You know from everyday life that it takes a strong,

secure person to admit error. True penitence doesn't stem from simply being aware of one's sin. The old-fashioned, fire-breathing, pulpit-pounding revivalists who tried to beat people into a sense of their own wretchedness understood neither psychology nor the gospel. Self-hatred and terror don't foster honesty.

Honesty, the kind which we pray for in worship, is the result of humility born of adoration. It flows from the security that "I am loved. God does care for me. God will not let me go."

I remember a child psychologist noting that any parent who stands over a four-year-old and booms, "Whoever stole those cookies from the cookie jar will be punished. Johnny, did you steal the cookies?" will elicit a lie from any intelligent child. Frightened, defensive people live by lies because they must. Without unconditional, unmerited, omnipotent love, what else can we be expected to do?

That's why the adoration and praise of this service has now led you and the congregation to the Prayer of Confession. The pastor calls people to confession, saying, "When we gather to praise God, we remember that we are God's people who have preferred our wills to God's will. Therefore, let us confess our sin before God and one another."

Then, with one voice, the church prays:

Merciful, God, we confess that often we have failed to be an obedient church:
    we have not done your will,
    we have broken your law,
    we have rebelled against your love,
    we have not loved our neighbors,
    we have not heard the cry of the needy.

Forgive us, we pray,
   Free us for joyful obedience,
   through Jesus Christ our Lord. Amen.
                 —From *We Gather Together*

The Sin of the Church

How do you feel about this prayer? Sometimes people say, "Those are not *my* sins. Why should I pray someone else's prayer?"

There is a prejudice abroad among many contemporary people that private religion is better than public religion, that private prayer is somehow more honest, more sincere, more heartfelt than public, corporate prayer. I shall have more to say about this matter of corporate prayer later. For now, let me note that we all pray this Prayer of Confession for two main reasons.

First, the sin being confessed here is the sin of the *church*. "We have failed to be an obedient church," we say. The bloodshed in so-called holy wars, the barbarity of the Crusades, the horrors of our anti-Semitism, the Inquisition, racial segregation in America and apartheid in South Africa, the wars between Protestants and Catholics in Northern Ireland, the imperialism of some Christian missionaries, our complicity in economic injustice, all are laid open to the scrutiny of a righteous God.

"The time has come for judgment to begin with the household of God" (1 Pet. 4:17). The very notion of sin implies some divine standard, some holy law which has been transgressed. Only communities of faith recognize divinity and holiness in the first place so only they are judged of sin. We see no sin in the world which has not been practiced with great expertise in the church. Because to us has been given the vocation of being "a light to the nations" (Isa. 42:6), the sin of God's own people is all the more appalling.

Our confession sets our worship in proper context. Dressed in our Sunday best, all washed and scrubbed, smiling and friendly, we are not as pure as we like to think we are. We admit that here, right here, at the very beginning, our hymns, our praying, processing, preaching are not some escape from reality, not some narcotic fantasy trip into never-never land. The confession keeps us tied to the facts. It is the fact of our sin, our infidelity, our falsehood which makes worship so desperately important for our survival.

Sometimes people outside our fellowship say, "The church is just a bunch of hypocrites." Here, at the beginning, we admit that we are a gathering of sinners, some of whom are hypocrites. We are no more embarrassed by this than the observation that hospitals are full of sick people. Long ago Jesus was criticized because, "This man receives sinners and eats with them" (Luke 15:2). He still does, every time the church gathers.

Second, if we have learned one thing in this century, it is that our most devastating sins are corporate in nature. Too often we think of sin the way we think of religion—as something which is purely personal and individual. Sin is smoking, drinking, sexual promiscuity. These sins damage us and our neighbors, that's true. But our social, corporate, systemic sin hurts whole neighborhoods. Our racism, nationalism, militarism, sexism are tough to control. Here, in the Prayer of Confession, we admit that our sins are but symptoms and expression of our Sin, our shared alienation from God. Our sin is a group product, a corporate phenomenon. The problem with the human species is not just that "every imagination of the thoughts of his heart was only evil continually" (Gen. 6:5), but that we perpetually go along with the crowd. Our sin seems to become worse when we are in a group. "Everyone else is doing it." The adolescent's plea has become the motto of a whole generation. Everyone else looks out for number one. Everyone else cheats on income tax forms. Everyone else plays loose with marriage vows. Therefore, this Prayer of Confession is not only the honest cry of the church but of the whole human race.

There is also a sense in which this public confession of our sin reminds us that honesty is a communal phenomenon. The person who is able to say, "I feel more religious when I stay at home on Sunday and watch a religious program on television," states what is true. In this isolated, individualized setting, it *is* easier to feel vaguely "religious." There's no one at home to challenge your cherished beliefs and prejudices, no one to disagree. The good friend who loves us so much that he or she is able to say, "Now, you and I both know that's not *really* the reason you did that," is a blessing, though a sometimes painful one. The church helps us to see ourselves as others see us, to hold up before us the mirror of corporate honesty. That's why, in the deepest sense, this is *my* prayer, *my* sin. True confession is as difficult to accomplish on our own as it is for a neurotic person to become cured without the aid of a therapist. It is not good for us to be alone (Gen. 2:18), especially alone with our sin.

The Prayer of Confession is a willingness to be known, to lay oneself open before God, to come,

"Just as I am, without one plea," to submit to the truth about ourselves and our church.

One thing which many of us enjoy about marriage is that marriage offers us the one relationship in life where we are able to be utterly honest. In the early days of a marriage we may think to ourselves, "I've got to be careful and be polite, patient, and caring." One feels as if one is on probation, since one so often is on probation within most human relationships. We therefore want to appear in the best light possible. But marriage is not just another human relationship. There eventually comes that time when we realize: "She is really here for good, loving me no matter who I am, in spite of who she knows me to be." For the first time, we are enabled to take off the masks, because she already knows the face behind the mask and has promised to love it and to live with it "for better, for worse, for richer, for poorer, in sickness and in health, until death us do part."

Confession is the liberating willingness to know ourselves as well as God knows us, warts and all. In confession we are not telling God anything that God doesn't know. We confess in order to express our acceptance of God's penetrating knowledge of us, our boldness (made bold because of God's love for us) to stand face-to-face with as much truth about ourselves as God's love enables us to bear.

The poet T. S. Eliot declared that humankind "cannot bear very much reality." On Sunday, we try for a stronger dose of reality than the world affords us. The Prayer of Confession is general enough to encompass all human sinfulness yet specific enough to make us squirm as we pray. Moving beyond a vague wish to somehow be better, we get down to specifics:

We have failed to be an obedient church:
    we have not done your will,
    we have broken your law,
    we have rebelled against your love,
    we have not loved our neighbors,
    we have not heard the cry of the needy.
          —From *We Gather Together*

Some time ago, I spoke to a group of seminary professors of pastoral counseling on "Theological Aspects of Divorce." In my talk, I suggested that divorce was an occasion for the church to offer forgiveness since divorce, the breaking of a promise, was a sin.

There was a great outcry. "I've known wonderful people who have divorced," said one counselor.

"Are you going to tell a woman who divorced her abusive husband that she is a sinner?" another asked.

The group rejected the idea that divorce was sinful. Divorce was a form of bereavement, they said, grief because of "the death of a relationship" rather than anxiety caused by sin.

What troubled me in our conversation was not their views on divorce (in spite of the teaching of Jesus and the church) but their inability to admit to the possibility of sin. I agree to the error of a church making divorce *the* great, unforgivable sin, but divorced people sin, married people sin, single people sin. A broken promise is wrong. It is a moral matter. A sin.

The attractiveness of the counselors' notion that divorce is a psychological problem of unresolved grief (rather than a moral matter) is that it rationalizes our behavior. A therapist tells you that you feel grief rather than guilt.

"I get the impression that you could not admit to the presence of sin in any human activity," I said. At first, I thought they had simply explained sin and evil away because it didn't fit into their psychotherapeutic theology—God the affirming Rogerian therapist.

Later I concluded that the problem was not an inability to admit to sin, but a loss of belief in God's grace. When a church loses confidence in the absolute, transcendent grace of God, what else can it do for its suffering souls than to rationalize our sin, moralize about our behavior, and keep assuring us that we are basically nice people who are doing the best we can? Without a story of redemption, if we are not doing our best, we are damned.

We are, in psychotherapist Scott Peck's phrase "people of the lie," building layer upon layer of self-deception, fearful to be honest, fleeing the light of self-exposure, the voice of conscience. No one need send us to hell; we are there, trapped in a web of self-delusion and dishonesty, victims of evil rather than victors.

The paradoxical affirmation of Christianity is that our admission of the presence of evil keeps evil from getting out of hand. Unable to confront our evil, we project, scapegoat, deny, rationalize, and destroy—sacrificing others rather than our delusions. That's why some of the most evil people are likely to be found in church—what better way to escape evil than to hide among the good? Can this be why some church people seem so hostile when confronted with the possibility of their own evil? They are in church to avoid rather than to encounter.

Yet it is my observation that the church is a dangerous place for those who deny evil. The church is a community of story, tradition, morality. In its own bumbling way, the church stumbles across the truth in spite of itself. People who devote their lives to denying their own imperfection, people who flee those situations where they will either be encouraged to self-examination or subject to the moral scrutiny of others, will eventually be unhappy in church.

Indeed the church could be characterized as that body of people who, in the name of Christ, continually battle evil, fighting it first within themselves, then tackling it in the world. If Scott Peck is right in *People of the Lie* (and I think he is) that "evil arises in the refusal to acknowledge our own sins," then the church is that truthful community which is always at war with evil, even as the battle lines are drawn here as we pray the Prayer of Confession. Sin is always narcissistic, the result, as Martin Luther said, of the "heart curved in upon itself," the tragic end of our fatal attempt to be God. So the church—when scripture is read, when an honest story is told, when a person is baptized—is placing itself at enmity with sin, desperately trying to wrench our gaze off ourselves in order to point us toward God. In so many ways, the church engages its people with the "over-againstness" of God, the otherness of reality which Isaiah encountered that day in the temple. God has made us free to look at the facts, or to turn away, so the success of the church is never assured. But whenever someone is converted, "born again" to the blessed and painful realization that we are "dust, and to dust . . . shall return," as well as forgiven, reconciled children of God, the church is about its proper business.

The church is not another self-help therapy group.

It is, particularly in its worship, prolonged training in humility, letting go of all attempts to seek help from the self. That day in the temple, Isaiah saw something which brought him to his knees. Worship is like that. In the beauty of God's presence, we see the banal, unimaginative quality of our sin. We go over the same confession week after week because sin, by its very nature, tends to be dull and unoriginal. The seven deadly sins of our forebears haven't been added to or improved upon by contemporary sinners. Our sin is appallingly monotonous so it is therefore fitting that our confession be a bit that way.

Rise, and Go in Peace

Now you see your pastor come and stand in full view of the congregation. With hands outstretched, the pastor says, in a loud, clear voice, "Hear the good news: 'Christ died for us while we were yet sinners; that is God's own proof of his love for us.' In the name of Jesus Christ, you are forgiven!"

Then you all respond, "In the name of Jesus Christ, you are forgiven!"

This reveals the whole purpose, the *Christian* point of our confession. Christians confess their sin, not simply to wallow in the mire of self-negation and despair, but that they might be free. Go through the Gospels and note how often Jesus says, "Your sins are forgiven." Jesus criticized those religious leaders of his day who heaped up burdens upon the backs of the people, turning religion into a burden rather than a blessing, but would do nothing to free them of their burdens.

To his disciples Jesus gave the awesome power to bind and to loose sin (John 20:23). "Truly, I say to you, whatever you bind on earth shall be bound in heaven, and whatever you loose on earth shall be loosed in heaven" (Matt. 18:18).

Our confession is not for the purpose of heroic acts of honesty but for being freed from the burden of our sin. Guilt is too big a burden for us to bear. Repentance is primarily an act of worship, not an act of self-recrimination or a wallowing in masochistic guilt feelings. Repentance in the Bible is *metanoia,* literally "turning." The call to repent is not simply a call to judgment but rather a call to, in the prophets' words, "return to the Lord." It is a turning away from ourselves back toward communion with one another and with God. In this turning is our liberation.

To be a community of truth, the church must be a community of forgiveness. Since we live in an imperfect world, still in the grip of sin, we must cope with our lapses. The kingdom isn't here yet, so we are ensnared in structures of sin over which we have no control. We pay taxes for unjust wars, we work for a political party whose stand on some issues we regard as racist, we accept the money of businesses that exploit the poor. We live under the dominion of sin and evil in the social order as well as in our private lives. No matter how hard we try, we can't avoid a sense of guilt. In fact, those among us who are most opposed to injustice will be those most convinced of our need to confess our unavoidable entanglement in injustice.

God acts not to condemn us but to forgive, to unclasp the iron bands that enslave the doer to the deed, to unlock the future. Through our confession, in the corporate Prayer of Confession, we articulate our guilt as well as our incapacity to overcome evil on our own. By God's word of pardon, we are freed from the burden of our guilt so that we may return to the front lines.

No one is much good in God's work who is there only to expiate guilt. The burden of guilt renders us weak, defensive, timid, and distracted. So the church offers us the blessedness of another human voice speaking. "Arise, and go in peace, your sins are forgiven."

Without such relief, without this Sunday-to-Sunday reassurance that ultimately it is not left up to us, that ultimately God is busy in us and in the world, we would despair. Reconciliation is essential to Christian persistence. As Jim White says in *Sacraments as God's Self-Giving:* "Without it, we are only a short-term militia, doomed to slink away in discouragement. But, because of reconciliation, we can enlist for a duration that lasts out our lifetime."

Now do you understand why the church's worship is a movement in the church's campaign against evil? There we receive what we need in order to give what it takes to be in this battle-weary army.

Jesus sent his first disciples to heal and cast out devils (Matt. 10:5-16). He still sends us, giving the church authority to do what he did throughout his ministry. After his resurrection, he breathed upon his disciples with the words, "Receive the Holy Spirit. If you forgive the sins of any, they are forgiven; if you retain the sins of any, they are retained" (John 20:22-23).

One reason that the lawyers hated Jesus was his readiness to pronounce forgiveness of sins, an act which seemed to them a blasphemous usurpation of God's power to forgive (Matt. 9:2-8). The scandal is that the church, that both sinful and saved body, is given this power.

The church is able to be a community of forgiveness because we forgive no sin in others which we have not asked God to forgive in us.

I always tell couples before their marriage, "One good thing about marriage is that it gives you lots of practice in forgiving and being forgiven." Marriage requires forgiveness because any intimate human relationship, any intimate divine-human relationship, can't endure long without forgiveness. So much of our sin is corporate, social, and public.

Our redemption is also corporate, social, and public. On our own, most of us cannot withstand the assault of evil. We get by with help from our friends who support us in the face of temptation, underscore our values, call us back to what is true, tell us the good news. The church is also the foretaste of the kingdom, a new human society where suffering, weakness, tragedy, and injustice are viewed differently from the way the world views these things. Here is a place to witness "a new heaven and a new earth," not as an isolated club of the elect, but as salt, light, and leaven to a dark world (Matt. 5:13-16; 13:33). Here is a colony, a bridgehead, where, at least in a preliminary way, "every rule and every authority and power" will be destroyed and Christ is putting "all his enemies under his feet," including that dreaded "last enemy" (1 Cor. 15:24ff.).

Alcoholics Anonymous is a good illustration of the necessity of the community in our struggles with evil. The worse the sickness, the more severe the depth of the evil, the more radical the cure. The AA group, in what can only be described as "tough love," leads the individual to admit that "we were powerless over alcohol—that our lives had become unmanageable." Then comes the infamous "Step Four": "We made a searching and fearless moral inventory of ourselves."

No such inventory could be attempted without the group. A church which is little more than a loose conglomeration of essentially self-interested individuals, half-heartedly committed either to discovery of the truth of Jesus or of themselves, is unlikely to be helpful in making moral inventories of self or society, much less finding a cure. We must do the tough congregational work of building a community strong enough to face the truth. Here, in praying the Prayer of Confession, we start down that hazardous and blessed road to freedom.

Note that your pastor stands in front of you to pronounce the Words of Pardon and Forgiveness. These words are spoken, "In the name of Christ." To say something in the name of someone is to speak with that person's authority, his blessing, in his behalf. The Words of Pardon should have come through as loud and clear, as firm and sure, as the Prayer of Confession—in fact, more so. Often it's much easier to believe that we are sinners than to believe that we are forgiven.

In today's service, the Prayer of Confession and the Words of Pardon and Forgiveness may come here, at the beginning of the service, in much the same way that Isaiah fell to his knees as soon as he saw the glory of God. But the confession-forgiveness acts could just as well occur after the sermon, after we have heard the word and have been confronted by it.

Traditionally the church forbade kneeling and other penitential acts in Sunday worship during seasons like Christmas and Easter because these were great festivals of joy when penitential acts seemed inappropriate. Therefore Sundays in Christmas and Easter are times when your church may wish to omit the Prayer of Confession, saving it for the traditionally penitential seasons of the church year such as Advent and Lent.

Now you rise to your feet, forgiven, reconciled, ready to hear the word and to serve God in worship. You say with those who have preceded you in the faith:

> My soul waits for the Lord
>> more than watchmen for the morning . . . .
>> O Israel, hope in the Lord!
>>> For with the Lord there is steadfast love,
>>> and with him is plenteous redemption.
>> And he will redeem Israel
>>> from all his iniquities.
>>>>> — Psalm 130:6-8

3.

Praise

*It is right to give
God thanks and praise.*

Praise the Lord!
Praise God in his sanctuary;
   praise him in his mighty firmament!
Praise him for his mighty deeds;
   praise him according to his exceeding
      greatness!

—Psalm 150:1-2

The organ blares forth; with the whole congregation you rise to your feet and sing,

> Glory be to our Creator,
> Praise to our Redeemer Lord,
> Glory be to our Sustainer,
> Ever three and ever one,
> As it was in the beginning,
> Now and ever more shall be.

This is the way people act when someone says, "Rise, your sin is forgiven." To be the recipient of such freedom is to rise to your feet and shout, "Amen!" That's what you are doing now—praising

53

God. People tend toward praise whenever they recognize God's presence.

Absence and Presence

Of course, God has been praised before in today's service. Your singing of the first hymn was an act of praise. Every "Amen!" in the service, every "Glory to God!" and your very presence here is praise.

There is a kind of alternating rhythm in worship between recognition of God's absence and experience of God's presence. We may not like to admit to the absence of God, yet it is as real as God's presence. In a life, even the most saintly life, there are always spaces, vacant places of the heart when God seems far away, remote. "Truly, thou art a God who hidest thyself" (Isa. 45:15). Even one so close to God as Jesus could cry out from the cross, "My God, my God, why hast thou forsaken me?" (Matt. 27:46). If God were never absent, it would make little sense to speak of God's presence. We don't often discuss the presence of oxygen. It's always there. But because God is the living God, the God who is able to declare, "My thoughts are not your thoughts, neither are your ways my ways" (Isa. 55:8), there will be times when God seems remote, absent. Biblical people speak as often of the hurt, forsakenness, and fear of God's absence as they celebrate God's presence. We can't tame, control, or domesticate God, even though sometimes our worship is a subconscious attempt to do so.

What was the Prayer of Confession a moment ago but an honest admission that in our church, our deeds, our lives, God is often absent? Partly this is so because of who God is—bigger than our concepts, institutions, ideals, righteousness. Partly this is so because of who we are—rebellious, dull, narcissistic. Sometimes God is absent because our prayers, our churches, our worship, our programs are so full of ourselves—our wants, our plans, our feelings—that there's no room left for God. We are busy asking ourselves in worship: Do I like this? Can I understand the point? Have we ever done this before? Will the preacher make me mad? How do I look? What's she doing here? There is no time left for God's questions: Where are you? Why are you here? What do you want?

At other times God is absent because there are places God can't go. That horrid child named "Ichabod" (meaning "gone is the glory"), whom Eli's daughter-in-law named for Israel when the nation's infidelity had caused God to leave, is sometimes us. In confessing our sin, we are confessing the absence of God in our lives. God is where justice is done; yet we tolerate injustice. God, the babe at Bethlehem reminds us, is with the poor and the outcast; yet we take the side of the rich and powerful. Little wonder that ours is an age and a culture in which the great plays, poems, and paintings of our time testify more to our experience of God's absence, the *deus absconditus*, the "hidden god," than to God's presence. We're all, like the characters in Samuel Beckett's play, sitting on a park bench *Waiting for Godot*—waiting for God. Is God absent because God no longer cares about us or because God has moved to where people still care about God?

A number of years ago, our divinity school was visited by Bishop Emilio Curvahallo of the Methodist Church in Angola. We were interested in how the church was surviving in a country which was ruled by a Marxist government. "We are doing fine," he said. "Our church is growing at the rate of about 10 percent per year, though some other denominations are growing even faster."

Had there been trouble with the government? "Yes, from time to time they pass laws that say we can't have this or that group meet. But we go ahead and keep meeting. The government is not yet strong enough to stop us."

But what will you do if the government becomes stronger? "We will keep meeting. It is their job to be the government, our job to be the church. Our church had its most rapid growth during the revolution when so many of our members were in jail. Jail is a wonderful opportunity for evangelism."

Then, perhaps realizing what was behind our questions, the bishop said, "Don't worry about us, brothers and sisters. We are doing fine in Angola. Frankly, I would find it much more difficult to be a pastor in Evanston, Illinois."

In our affluence, indifference, and comfort perhaps we don't need God as much as other people do— where there is suffering, persecution, hunger, and poverty. So God seems absent to us.

That is why, in the midst of our singing, praying, speaking, and reading in worship there needs to be some time for silence. Yet silence is peculiarly threatening. Have you noticed our tendency to fill up all the empty spaces in worship with the preacher's chatter or the organist's syrupy interludes? It is as if we are almost frightened by silence so the preacher keeps chattering, "Now, please get your bulletins and let us all turn to the next hymn, that great hymn of Charles Wesley, and let us all stand as we sing, 'O for a thousand tongues to sing, my great Redeemer's praise.' "

There must be absence before there can be presence. At times we must leave behind our sounds, chatter, and music so that there is room for God to come. Are we afraid that, in our silences, God might come and surprise us? Is that why we keep talking and moving and singing?

There may be a good deal more experience of God's absence in the lives of people who sit beside you in the pew than we admit. The unanswered prayers, sad lives, unexplained tragedies, and general dismay at the way the world sometimes works fill them with a sense of being alone, bereft.

Besides, let us honestly confess that even as we long for God's presence, we also fear it. Rather than expose our lives to the glare of God's judgment, better to keep them safely compartmentalized—religion is what you do in church on Sunday; life is politics, economics, business, marriage, what you do Monday through Saturday. Better leave God at the church door as we exit, tucked safely in the sanctuary until next Sunday, than to suffer God's incursions into our daily lives. Sunday sometimes functions as much to protect us from God's presence as to end God's absence. Do we really desire that God should be here?

A professor of mine has much contact with his counterparts in the Soviet Union. He told me that his friendship with a Soviet professor had made him look at many things differently.

"In what way do you look at things differently?" I asked.

"Have you ever met an honest-to-goodness atheist?" he asked me. "I mean a person who is an atheist the way you are a Methodist, a person who has been an atheist since childhood, brought up that way."

I said that I had not. "What makes her different?" I asked.

"That's just the point," he said. "She isn't different. She is really no different in her conversation, morality, and outlook than an average American. She makes her decisions, spends her money, decides on what she will do tomorrow the same way that I do. When it comes down to it, we're all atheists. It's as natural as the air we breathe in modern life—we all live as if God doesn't matter."

The Work of Praise

But now, as you rise to your feet, the rhythm of presence/absence merges into presence. Exposing yourself to the possibility of divine presence, you have not been disappointed. "Glory be to our Creator,/Praise to our Redeemer Lord."

Sometimes, at this point, an anthem may be sung, or a hymn. Whatever is done now, this is an act of praise. As you stand and sing, there is something within you that tells you this is what Sunday is all about. This is why you are here, why we all are here, so that we might come to the point where God's love and God's care and God's presence might be so real that we rise to our feet and sing.

So much of our time in church is spent discussing words like *should* and *ought* and *must*. Sunday is the day to heap on the burden of greater responsibility to be borne the rest of the week, the day when the preacher tells us what we ought to do, the day when we admit to all the ways that we have, in the words of the old confession, "done those things which we

ought not to have done and have not done those things which we ought to have done."

Praise soars above this prosaic language of obedience, command, and obligation. Praise is an expression of abundance rather than need, a time when we are able to say with the psalmist, "my cup runneth over." Praise arises like laughter, spontaneously, welling up within us until we can sit and be silent no longer. Without denying the reality of God's absence in much of our life, we can admit to the reality of God's presence in much of our life. Now is the time to celebrate the presence.

What you are doing now is best described in the words of the old Westminster Catechism when it asks, "What is the chief end of man?" The response: "to glorify God and to enjoy him forever."

In praise we are fulfilling our chief purpose in life, the main reason why the Creator has placed us upon this planet—not to obey, or even to serve but rather to enjoy! Remember that one of the chief charges against Jesus was that he was "a glutton and drunkard" (Matt. 11:19). His critics were shocked by Jesus' enjoyment of God and people: "The disciples of John fast often and offer prayers, and so do the disciples of the Pharisees, but yours eat and drink" (Luke 5:33). We can tell that John's disciples are religious—they look so miserable! After all, what is the purpose of religion if not to be miserable? But Jesus' disciples eat and drink. Jesus' response? "When the bridegroom arrives for the wedding party, do the guests look sad? No! The bridegroom is here. Let the party begin!" (Luke 5:34-35, AP).

Our praise, our joy, is joy in response to the presence. The Lord is here, among us. Joy is invariably reflexive, responsive. We can't *decide* to be joyful. Joy is not something we do. It is rather the fitting response to the action of someone else upon us. When a rocket explodes, illuminating a July sky, showering brilliant sparks, an "Ah!" of wonder arises from the crowd. The crowd is beyond the realm of reason, decision, and choice. Their "Ah!" is response to an event, a happening, a presence. Joy is like that. It is not a warm, rosy feeling we work up—to do so would be artificial, forced. Joy, holy joy, is reflexive. To be here on Sunday is to place ourselves where joy, real joy is possible.

When we praise we join "all the company of heaven" in their song of unending praise. We experience our chief purpose in life—to enjoy God forever. As C. S. Lewis says, "Joy is the serious business of heaven." Here, on Sunday morning, for moments within this hour of worship, we are rehearsing the parts that we shall play in heaven, glorifying and enjoying God forever. Doxology is the serious business of the church.

In fact, the great theologian Karl Barth says in his *Church Dogmatics* (IV) that praise is the mark of the true church:

All ministries, whether of speech or action, are performed well to the extent, that they all participate in the praise of God. The praise of God which constitutes the community and its assembly, seeks to bind and commit and therefore to express, well up and surge in concert. The Christian community sings from inner material necessity. What we can and must say quite confidently is that the community that does not sing is not the community.

This challenges the notion that to adore God we must abase ourselves. When we confess our sins, we are admitting that this sin is not an inherent part of who God created us to be. In praise, we are being who we are—namely, beloved children. Praise is best done as a hymn, an anthem, poetry, music. Prose is usually too confining for the joyful business we are about here. We are, in this moment, in the words of the old hymn, "lost in wonder, love, and praise." You may have come here this morning wondering, What does God want me to do with my life? What ought I to do tomorrow morning? How do I look, here in church? Now, all that is quite beside the point. Our gaze has been wrenched off ourselves, our problems, our thoughts of ought and should and must. By adoration we have moved beyond mere thinking, planning, evaluating or self-conscious posturing. There is a sense that here, in praise, worship is really worship.

Whenever I discuss worship with people, I am impressed by how many folk feel guilty about their worship. "I can't keep my mind on what's going on," someone may say. "My mind wanders to what I am to do after the service or what we are having for dinner. I can't concentrate on the prayers or the sermon."

Or someone else says, "I find myself just going through the motions, saying the Lord's Prayer, not thinking about what I am doing."

To these troubled people I want to say, "Relax! Enjoy! You are not here to *do* anything. You are not supposed to be thinking, changing, doing. You are here simply to 'glorify God and to enjoy him forever.'" There is something about worship that is ruined when you work too hard at it.

A young man falls in love with a young woman. He

begins to whistle a tune as he walks down the sidewalk. Then he sings. He believes that he has never
seen a day more beautiful than today, the sky, the
trees, the people. Now he is skipping, almost danc-
ing down the sidewalk.

"Young man, do you know what you are doing?"
someone asks. "What good will all this singing, danc-
ing, and joy do you?"

What a silly, impertinent question to ask of someone who is in love. Of course he doesn't *know* what he
is doing, and that's just the fun of it. As my friend
John Westerhoff has said, "If you have to think about
it, it isn't good worship." What we are doing here is
infinitely deeper, more engaging, more involved than
mere thinking. To merely think about it, as a detached
observer cooly analyzing everything, is an irrelevant,
irreverent way to be in love or in worship. Worship is
a way of being in love, of glorifying and enjoying the
One of whom we can say, "We love, because he first
loved us" (1 John 4:19).

The beginnings of praise are present in most lives,
implicitly, incipiently: The "Ah!" that rises from our
lips when a skyrocket bursts in a July evening sky, the
hush that comes over us when we stand on the sum-
mit and look across a hazy, blue mountain valley, the
tear that comes to our eyes when we hold our child
for the first time in our arms. Praise is being who we
really are, fulfilling our chief end, our main purpose
in life. It is as natural as breathing for children to
jump and shout for joy when they hear that a circus is
coming to town. Praise is as natural as falling in love,
walking on the beach at sunset, and embracing someone who is dear to us. Praise moves beyond words,
quickly becoming music or dance.

Praise is a means of loving, an expression of what we value most and whom we love the most. Praise is a means to loving, a way of deepening our relationship to the One in whom we live and move and have our being" (Acts 17:28). We kiss because we are in love. We kiss in order to be in love. The act of affection both expresses where we are and moves us to where we wish to be. Praise is like that.

In life or in worship, praise is often spontaneous, fresh, unexpected, like the "Ah!" that comes in response to something wonderful. That's probably why some people resent being asked to be joyful on Sunday morning, even when they may not feel like being joyful. To them it seems contrived, artificial, and forced to be told to confess, thank, praise as if these things should happen on cue, according to what's printed in the bulletin.

Unfortunately, this matter of being in love, which is, as we have said, related to the matter of praising God, is not so simple that it can be limited to the utterly spontaneous. In life the "Ah!" of joy and wonder is a spontaneous phenomenon, sometimes catching us offguard, surprising us. Yet we do take trips to the beach, and climb mountains, and pick flowers, and go to concerts because we have found it wise to put ourselves where such spontaneous experiences often do occur. Sunday morning in church is partly an attempt to put ourselves in the place where the spontaneity happens.

"I can worship God as well on the golf course as in church," someone says. Well, yes, but is that why people go to golf courses? How often does worship take place on a golf course? It's not the time, not the place. Time and place make a difference.

Keeping at it also makes a difference. I remember meeting an avant-garde couple in seminary who told me that they had decided to raise their child free of restrictive social conventions and artificial restraints.

"For instance," the husband said, "we are not going to teach our son such worn out customs as 'Say thank you to the nice lady.' We will let him express gratitude spontaneously, as it arises within him rather than because mommy and daddy taught him to do it."

You guessed it. In a year or so of observation of this child I can honestly say that I never once heard the child say "please" or "thank you." What I observed was a spoiled, self-centered, unruly brat. Human emotions like gratitude, selflessness, courtesy—emotions which make us *human*—are not inborn. They must be cultivated, nurtured, habitualized within us. One of the chief duties of parents is to teach their children good habits—saying thank you, waiting your turn, showing respect for the feelings of others. These traits don't come naturally.

Most of us eat, sleep, work, make love out of habit. We habitualize certain actions because we think they are important. Most Christians go to church out of habit. Contrary to popular belief, their habit in no way minimizes the importance of this experience, in fact, it confirms its importance. Spontaneity is fine, so far as it goes. But our deepest feelings, our most important values and commitments, must be constantly reiterated in our lives. Therefore we do them out of habit.

Show me a married couple who decide to kiss one another only when they each feel a deep, spontaneous, overwhelming need to do so, and I will show you a sick marriage! Married couples learn that there are some things which are too important to be left to chance. There are things which we do for one another because the other person needs it, because we need to be kept close to the things and the people we value most.

Show me a Christian who only goes to church when he or she feels a deep, spontaneous, over-whelming need to praise God, and I will show you a rather weak, insubstantial disciple. Praise may be as natural as breathing, but we need to keep at it, like the stories Jesus told about prayer, about the woman who hounded the judge until he gave her what she wanted (Luke 18:1-8) and the man who pounded upon his friend's door at midnight until his friend got out of bed and gave him bread for his guest (Luke 11:5-13). We are to be persistent. Keep at it.

Let's be honest. Some Sundays we feel like praise and some Sundays we don't. Some Sundays we feel very close to God and very grateful for God's gifts to us and some Sundays—we would rather be back home sleeping late. That's the way we are. And that's all right. But because that is the way we are, we humans need times when we put ourselves in the right place at the right time in order to do what we truly want to do and be whom we truly want to be.

I remember a sermon in which the minister asked all husbands and wives in the congregation to turn to their husband or wife and "tell him or her one reason why you love them." People were embarrassed. It seemed forced, contrived. Yet, when you did it, you really did feel more loving. There was something about the act of verbalizing one's feelings, letting the other persons hear it. Something important happened to both the one who spoke and the one who listened.

All of this is to say that while praise is an inherently spontaneous activity, it can arise out of those hymns, prayers, and moments in worship when we are invited to praise, given vehicles to express what we may feel, but don't even know that we feel until we are given the means of expression. We stand and sing, "Glory be to our Creator,/Praise to our Redeemer Lord." And we are glorifying and enjoying God, in spite of ourselves. We are expressing how we really feel, glad to have the opportunity to reclaim our true selves, our real feelings in this act of praise.

Life as Praise

Of course, there is always a danger that, in worship, our praise might become an end in itself. This is the danger when worship becomes the exuberant "high," a mere "trip" into some fantasy world which has nothing whatsoever to do with the real world. There are some styles of worship which are frankly escapist, pure ecstasy and little else. People come in to worship, get all happy, excited, and emotional, then put back on their coats and hats and go back to the real world.

This doesn't seem to be a Methodist problem! In my tradition, we tend to be preoccupied with busyness, intercession, self-improvement, self-conscious activism, breathless activity. Church is where you come, not to praise God, to glorify and enjoy God, but where you come to get your list of assignments to work on for next week: work on improving your marriage, try to be kind to your business partners, get your social attitudes cleaned up.

Here, in this act of praise, is the antidote to this rather (if I may use such a strong phrase) a-theistic conception of Sunday worship. Praise is response to the loving presence of God. Without that presence, we might as well turn the church into a self-improvement class, a lecture on ancient religion, or a pep rally for our latest social justice cause. Alas, this is what church has too often become for many of our people.

Praise is the applause of the church. It is our experience of ourselves at our best, our most fitting response to the presence of God in our lives. As the old service of Holy Communion puts it, the minister says to the people, "Lift up your hearts." The people respond, "It is meet and right, so to do." The "meet" here is the old English way of saying that it is "fitting." It is fitting that we should "at all times and places" lift up our hearts to God. It is fitting that we should do so, everywhere, everytime; but we need this opportunity here, in church, in worship to be reminded that praise is the very purpose of our lives.

One Easter a man left my church at the end of the service saying, "If I die right now, it's OK." Admittedly, moments like that don't happen everyday. But when they do, we realize that we are at the very heart of the matter. We are swept up into "wonder, love, and praise," and we know that, no matter where we go from here or whatever happens to us after this moment, we are all right.

Yet this does not mean that the Christian life ends here, in this time of ecstasy and exuberant abandon. Our chief end is to glorify and enjoy God. But this is using "end" in the sense of "purpose" rather than finality. Our purpose is praise. We are, in the words of Paul, to present our bodies, our whole life, to God as our gift (Rom. 12:1). A Christian, in a sense, doesn't recognize a difference between life in church and life on the outside. All life, our worship or our work, is our attempt to praise God. Our ethics are similar to our singing—offering ourselves and our gifts to God. If cultivated in worship, praise flows back into everyday life. We become better at praising God, more responsive to the presence of God in church or out.

Why do Christians care about ecology and our environment? Because we have sung "this is my father's world" in our worship. Why do Christians have certain strong opinions about war, peace, capital punishment, poverty, racism, sexism, and hunger? Because we have prayed with the angels, "Glory to God in the highest, and on earth peace among men" (Luke 2:14).

How do you make good people? One Christian response is that you form good people by first teaching them to praise God, by bidding them to turn around and look in the right direction, to open their eyes to the presence of God in all things. Christian goodness flows from Christian love. Our ethics are always doxological, a natural response of a people who know how to look at their lives and the world and sing:

> Praise God, from whom all blessings flow;
> Praise him, all creatures here below;
> Praise God above, ye heavenly host;
> Praise Father, Son, and Holy Ghost.

Perhaps this is how Paul can urge us to, "always

seek to do good to one another and to all. Rejoice always, pray constantly, give thanks in all circumstances" (1 Thess. 5:15-18). Note that Paul links our behavior toward one another with our prayer and praise of God. They go together.

Christians may differ on their approach to various social, moral, and ethical issues. Our goal is not total agreement with one another, or affirmation of what is permissible and possible. Our goal is to fashion our attitudes, actions, and lifestyles in such a way that the world is able to look at us and see a hymn of praise. We may disagree on the words to that hymn, yet we agree that, in the words of Paul again, "whether you eat or drink, or whatever you do, do all to the glory of God" (1 Cor. 10:31; Rom. 14:6).

4.

Scripture

This is the word of the Lord.

He came to Nazareth, where he had been brought up; and he went to the synagogue, as his custom was, on the sabbath day. And he stood up to read; and there was given to him the book of the prophet Isaiah. He opened the book and found the place where it was written . . .

—*Luke 4:16-17.*

As the congregation is seated, Jane Smith moves up from the congregation to the lectern. Jane says, "Please pray the Prayer for Illumination with me." All pray, "O Lord, open our hearts and minds by the power of your Holy Spirit so that as the scriptures are read and the word proclaimed, we might hear with joy what you say to us today. Amen."

Jane then opens the large Bible on the lectern, the one which the Bible bearer brought in at the beginning of the service, finds her place, and announces, "The first lesson is from the prophet Isaiah."

The Church's Book

Some time ago, your pastor began the practice of

71

using three lessons from scripture each Sunday: A lesson from the Hebrew scriptures, an epistle lesson, and one from the Gospels. She explained how this was an ancient practice in the church. While you have always been in favor of people having a better knowledge of the Bible, you are not sure of how you feel about having this much scripture in the Sunday service.

Part of your reason for feeling this way about the lessons is that you are not too sure of what to do while all three lessons are being read. You try to pay attention, to do your best to comprehend and remember all the lessons, but it isn't easy. It's one thing to read scripture at home, in your own Bible study and meditation, but another thing to try to concentrate here in church. You wonder if all of this reading might be more appropriate at some other time. What is the purpose of scripture reading on Sunday morning?

The question is an important one for those of us in the Protestant tradition. Our spiritual forebears were convinced that the Bible was the very source of the church's vitality. The Protestant Reformation began, in great part, as a movement to restore scripture to its central place in the life of the church and the church's worship. The United Methodist *Book of Discipline 1980* puts it this way:

> United Methodists share with all other Christians the conviction that Scripture is the primary source and guideline for doctrine. The Bible is the deposit of a unique testimony to God's self-disclosures: in the world's creation, redemption and final fulfillment; in Jesus Christ as the incarnation of God's Word; in the

Holy Spirit's constant activity in the dramas of history. It is the primitive source of the memories, images, and hopes by which the Christian community came into existence and that still confirm and nourish its faith and understanding.

Yet in too many contemporary Protestant churches, the words of scripture have taken a backseat to psychological exhortations, catchy lyrics in bouncy songs, and the superficiality of grinning, backslapping conviviality. Snippets of scripture are read, usually from the pastor's favorite passages, as a mere springboard for a sermon which may or may not have much to do with the plain sense of the text.

It is no wonder that many of our congregations feel rootless, confused, and unsure of who they are or what they should be doing. They have been cut off from the rudder which holds the church on course.

When the Bible is read in public worship, as Jane is doing in your service now, the Bible is being restored to its original context. The church arose out of the synagogue, where worship was mainly a matter of speaking and listening to scripture. The Bible was never intended to be read silently, in the confines of our own homes. When we read it thus today, that's fine. But the original purpose of scripture, the only way that the majority of Christians ever heard it, was orally, in the corporate worship of the church.

Here is a glimpse at this Jewish dynamic of speaking and listening which gave birth to the Christian faith:

He came to Nazareth, where he had been brought up;

and he went to the synagogue, as his custom was, on the sabbath day. And he stood up to read; and there was given to him the book of the prophet Isaiah. He opened the book and found the place where it was written,
"The Spirit of the Lord is upon me,
because he has anointed me to preach good news to the poor.
He has sent me to proclaim release to the captives
and recovering of sight to the blind,
to set at liberty those who are oppressed,
to proclaim the acceptable year of the Lord."
And he closed the book, and gave it back to the attendant, and sat down; and the eyes of all in the synagogue were fixed upon him. And he began to say to them . . . .
—*Luke 4:16–21*

The function of sabbath worship was to open the scriptures, to sit at the feet of the rabbi as the traditions of the community were interpreted and thus brought to life. On that day at Nazareth, Rabbi Jesus was handed the scroll. He read the ancient words, known by every faithful person there, then he set these words in the context of the present. Your church does the same today in its reading and preaching.

We believe that the synagogue, with its Service of the Word, originated during Israel's exile. What do people do when they are strangers in a strange land? They tell stories so that people do not forget where home is. They tell stories to their young so that they will know who they are. They sing the old songs and rehearse again their values, their beliefs.

Today, in your church, when we read and interpret scripture, we are reliving the faith of Israel, the faith that the word continually creates a people who are capable of surviving in an alien world. The American world has generally been friendly to the American church. But when we listen to scripture, we see that all popular American values are not necessarily Christian values. Our children spend an average of four hours every day in front of a television set. They are not merely being entertained. They are being instructed, carefully informed and trained into the ways of an ideology which is alien to much of the gospel.

How will our children have faith unless we are intentional about witnessing to the truth of our faith? How will we survive, as Christians unless we are attentive to the word? So in today's world, the church finds that it is taking the Bible with a new seriousness, a new sense of urgency.

The Bible is the church's book. It is the result of Israel's and then the church's attempt to let God be God. Every word of scripture has as its main audience the church. The Bible is our best friend, our most severe critic. The tough task of being a Christian is the tough task of forming a community which is worthy to be a partner in the divine-human dialogue which is the Bible.

All this explains why, when we come to the reading of scripture in Sunday worship, we are at the very center of our worship. This story is our story, the source of our identity, the wellspring of our life together.

My church reads three lessons each Sunday in continuity with ancient practice. These lessons come from something which is called a lectionary. A lectionary is a table of scripture readings for every Sunday of the year. My church uses the new Common

Lectionary which lists readings on a three-year cycle. Roman Catholics, United Methodists, Lutherans, Presbyterians, Episcopalians, and the United Church of Christ are among the many denominations which use the Common Lectionary. Unfortunately, many factors still divide the body of Christ. Isn't it good to know that we can at least agree on the centrality of scripture? All over town, Christians gather on Sunday and listen to the same lessons which you hear read.

Usually your pastor will preach from one of these lessons, but not always. The main reason to read these lessons is that God's people ought to hear God's word. It is as important to hear scripture as to hear words about the scripture. Use of the lectionary helps worship planners to coordinate music in the service and to structure the service in such a way that it has unity and direction. Preachers also find that the lectionary helps them avoid simply going over their own pet themes again and again in sermons. Reading three lessons reminds us that we honor the whole Bible not just our favorite passages. All of us pick and choose certain portions of scripture for special emphasis, often based upon what we like and what we agree with. The lectionary disciplines us to confront a wider range of scripture than we might if we were left to our own choice in the matter. Congregations appreciate that their preacher's sermons arise not simply from the preacher's pet themes but from the full range of the demands of scripture.

Added to our concern that we read from a wider array of scripture through use of the Common Lectionary is a new concern for exposure to a wider array of images within scripture through the use of more inclusive biblical images.

The Bible is the product of its time and place—a patriarchal culture where women were subservient to men in society. The Bible both participates in this unjust patriarchy and also gives us the means to free ourselves from such injustice. God is called a father by Jesus—but is also compared to a mother hen protecting her chicks. We are surprised (considering the time and place of the Bible) to find women numbered among the first followers of Jesus. In fact, the Jesus story beings with a woman, Mary, being courageously obedient to the will of God.

This same sense of the inclusiveness of the Good News for all people should permeate our scripture reading and interpretation. The Bible pushes us to search for new means of speaking to more people—including everyone in the promise of salvation, excluding no one on the basis of our language.

When all our images concern men, we may have excluded over half the average congregation. When our language, pronouns, and metaphors imply that only adult, healthy, relatively affluent males are recipients of the gospel, we have blasphemously distorted the heart of the Bible's witness to Christ.

The Function of Scripture

Back to your earlier question: What is the purpose of our scripture reading on Sunday morning?

First, this is our history. A Christian is a Christian, in great part, because he or she is someone who has listened to this story. The church has no other legitimate means of obtaining its values, its identity, and its peculiar point of view. We must not forget how strange is the point of view of faith. Think of all the

times when you have heard the Bible read and you
find yourself muttering, "Where in the world do they
get that?" or "I never heard that before," or "How
strange!"

A man had two sons, one was a hard-working,
obedient boy. The other left home and squandered
his inheritance in loose living. When the prodigal
returned home, the father threw a party to welcome
him back.

An owner of a vineyard hired some people to work
for him early one morning. Later in the day the
owner went again into the marketplace and hired
more workers. Late in the afternoon he hired still
more. At the end of the day, when the wages were
paid, the owner paid those who had worked only one
hour as much as he paid those who had labored
all day.

On and on the stories go. How strange they are.
Here is the God who said of old, "My thoughts are
not your thoughts, neither are your ways my ways"
(Isa. 55:8). The Bible keeps us in touch with that
strangeness, keeps us aware of the distance between
our way of looking at things and God's way of looking
at things.

To listen to scripture is to be confronted with a
vision of a new heaven and a new earth. It is to be
given, as it were, new lenses through which we see a
very different kind of world. Our vision becomes dull.
We eventually see only what we want to see, only what
we think is possible, permissible. When we open the
scriptures, our world view is cracked open, the mists
clear, and we see things in new ways.

Jesus often used stories and images to help his disciples see things in a new and unexpected way. One day

Jesus and his disciples were walking along the road. When they arrived at Capernaum, he asked his disciples, "What were you discussing on the way?"

The disciples were silent because they had been in a row over who would be greatest in the kingdom. "When we get him elected Messiah and the campaign is over," they had said, "who will get to sit on the cabinet?"

In response to them, Jesus put a child in the midst of them. He took the child in his arms and said, "Whoever receives a child like this, receives me" (Mark 9:33-37, AP).

The disciples had been arguing about who was the greatest; Jesus responded by forcing them to look at the least, the lowest, the smallest. Previously he had told them that the first shall be last and the last shall be first, that he or she who would be the greatest of all must be smallest of all. Jesus himself is the very least of all, the child. He is, like a child, a little one as the world measures greatness. He is weak, vulnerable, and powerless.

This episode is reminiscent of another occasion when Jesus was speaking to the disciples—everyone was taking notes as Jesus lectured, trying to pay attention, trying to get the point—and they said to Jesus, "Send these noisy children away. We can't pay attention with them here."

Jesus beckoned the children forward and said, "Let the little children come to me, for of such is the kingdom of God" (Mark 10:13-14, AP).

He put a child in the midst of them, not to distract them, but to help them pay attention, to help them see how one enters this strange, countercultural kingdom. To enter this door, one must be small, lowly, weak, needy. Of course, in the world, to be poor, unemployed, terminally ill, very young, very old, very retarded, very unsuccessful is to be a nobody. But in this kingdom, one has to be small, lowly to get in. Everybody gets to be little someday. God's power is manifested among the poor, the sick, the hungry, the children, the lowly. Here is a new kind of king and a new kingdom which belongs to little ones.

Ever since Jesus put this child in the middle of his disciples, the church is unable to look at the poor, the sick, the hungry, the children, the lowly as the world looks at those people because we have now been taught to view them as God does. By contemporary, secular standards, the church has some peculiar ideas about those who are the most vulnerable arising out of our peculiar point of view.

So, a main task of the church is simply to pay attention to these stories, to let them have their way with us, to instruct us in what to see, what to value, what to work for, what to wish for, pray for, wait for.

Another reason we listen to scripture is as a helpful antidote to the merely contemporary in our lives. We Americans have been called "neophiles," lovers of the new. We sell cars with the claim that this is the "new and improved model." If it's new, it's got to be improved, so the reasoning goes. People therefore participate in the old stories, ancient rituals, and archaic dress and language of the church and ask if all this is relevant. What they usually mean is, What can I do with all of this today?

The church, with its Sunday morning vestments, ancient books, odd language, and old-fashioned ways is sometimes embarrassed by being out of step with the spirit of the age. There have been times in the history of the church when the church completely lost touch with its surrounding culture, so much so that it was utterly unable to reach that culture with the gospel. The church thus failed in its missionary task by withdrawing into an archaic club of religiously inclined antiquarians who enjoyed handling old things.

But today one wonders if the church is so enmeshed in the surrounding culture that we are unable to reach that culture with the gospel. There is a strange relevance in irrelevance. Sometimes in our earnest attempt to speak to the world, we fall in. The church adopts a chameleon-like stance, blending in with our surroundings so that the church and its witness are indistinguishable from the prevalent thought of the age.

Someone has said that a church which marries the spirit of this age is destined to be a widow in the next. The history of the church contains periods when the church lost touch with the world by withdrawing into itself in self-contented isolation. However, there are more periods in church history when the problem was not how to relate to the surrounding world but how to keep the world from subverting the church.

As a young pastor, Reinhold Niebuhr expressed shame when he realized how the church of his day, to a great extent, capitulated to the hysteria of the First World War and fell into step with nationalistic vilification of the Germans and self-righteous posturing of the Allies rather than attempting to offer a word of sanity to the situation. He decided that, in great part, the church was so frightened at being left behind as the nation moved into the excitement of war, that it mindlessly climbed upon the bandwagon, blessing American militarism and nationalism at the expense of the gospel.

Much of the church's worship is admittedly old-fashioned, traditionalist, and antiquarian—and should be. The church may have some odd views of what it means to be truly relevant to this culture. Sometimes the best thing we can give our world is the gift of remembrance. Note how often the prophets of ancient Israel called upon the people to remember. "Return! Return!" they cried. In times of national prosperity and pride, the prophets reminded Israel that its affluence came as a gift of God. Great gifts imply great responsibilities. In times of national defeat and despair, the prophets reminded Israel of God's mercy and justice in the past. Remembrance gave hope in dark days.

The modern mind, limited to the confines of its own immediate experience, unable to envision a hopeful future because it doesn't know enough of the past to see beyond the trials of today, is ill equipped to stride into tomorrow. Too many of us can see only that which has happened to us personally. We are therefore plagued by facile optimism which superficially believes that everything will turn out right, in spite of what we do today, or a sophomoric pessimism which cynically decides that the world is going straight to hell because we know so little of what has happened in the past.

Recently I heard a psychiatrist discussing the growing problem of adolescent suicide. One of his theories for the cause of teenage suicide is that, in his words, "Kids have no history. They therefore have no perspective, no way to take the long view of their problems. When you break up with your girlfriend, this may seem like the end of the world because your world is so small. Problems are magnified and quickly engulf the fragile, insecure personality of the adolescent. In such circumstances, suicide seems the only way out."

Like the Jews before us, Christians are called to return, to remember, and take heart. Remembrance gives all of us perspective (literally, in Latin, "to see through") so that we are enabled to see through present events to some larger purpose and meaning. So we spend a good deal of time in worship repeating the promises, going back over the old stories, and rehearsing the drama which is faith, this continuing dialogue between God and humanity. Scripture is our primary means of remembering.

The church also reads scripture because this book is our canon for judging between our own faithfulness or infidelity. Many modern people are searching for more enduring values. When our only value is self-centeredness, no wonder so many of us are lonely. When our only goal in life is financial security, no wonder that so many are bored. When our only desire is the fulfillment of desire, no wonder that we are forever feeling empty. In life we often get what we want and too many of us have wanted far too little from life.

A church is judged, not by its size, its success in attracting new members or running a multiplicity of programs and activities. A church is judged solely by its faithfulness to scripture. As the Bible says, judgment always begins with the household of God. The Bible is our friend but also our most severe critic. Time and again in our history, this critical friend has called us to task and, in so doing, put us back on the path of discipleship.

Of course, you know enough about the Bible to know that the Bible is no mere rule book which will tell you or the church what to do on every possible subject. I think of the Bible more as a compass pointing us in the right direction than a road map telling us exactly which turn to take next. The Bible doesn't answer all our questions; in fact, it may leave us with even more questions. But the Bible does put us in the proper context whereby we may learn to ask new questions and to be prepared for new and startling answers. The Bible creates a peculiar people who expect to be surprised by the commands of God, a people who humbly listen.

There you sit on Sunday morning, listening to the words from this ancient book. You are just listening in on God's conversation with someone else, some ancient, Near Eastern person who doesn't resemble you at all. Then zap, when you least expect it, you hear the word as if it were spoken directly to you, and these ancient words become your word from God. You feel your life set apart, exposed, measured by some standard more worthwhile than the ones by which you often judge yourself.

That's why the church has traditionally spoken of the Bible as the canon for the church, yardstick by which the church measures life. People may say of the church that we are being "un-American" or "old-fashioned" or "radical" or "conservative" or "unpatriotic" and the church will barely take notice of such criticism. But if someone were to say that we were being "unbiblical," it would be a much more serious, much more damning charge against the church and one which cuts at the very heartbeat of our lives.

How does the church measure up when a Jane Smith stands, opens the ancient book, and reads from scripture?

A story is read about Jesus putting the little child in the midst of the disciples and saying, "Whoever receives one such child in my name receives me" (Matt. 18:5).

The church immediately asks itself: Where are our children? Do we remove our children from the Sunday worship service? What does this story say about that? Are children placed at the center or on the periphery of this congregation?

Or the stories are read of Jesus commanding Peter to put away his sword rather than take up arms against Caesar's soldiers, not to resist the onslaughts of the evil one. We see our own Lord hanging upon the cross, suffering injustice rather than taking up arms against it, and suddenly all of our discussion about violence, about capital punishment, about war and peace are put into new perspective. Much of our conventional reasoning crumbles before the image of a Savior who saves by suffering. We see things differently.

Preparing for the Word

You already know that listening is aided by preparation. Therefore, in order to get more out of this aspect of worship, you may need to put more into it. If your church uses the lectionary as a source for its Sunday scripture reading and preaching, ask your pastor for a copy of the lectionary and then read the assigned lessons at home before you come to church on Sunday.

There are a growing number of devotional resources which are tied to the lectionary, such as *The Upper Room Disciplines*. Using these aids for devotion, you will come to worship already primed for attentive hearing of the scriptures.

Some people find it helpful to bring their own Bible to church and to follow along in their Bible as the scripture is read. Some churches place Bibles in the pew racks. Personally, I prefer simply to listen as the word is read. There is a special quality to hearing scripture read. Each time scripture is read aloud, the reader interprets and enlivens the word simply by the way he or she reads it.

Recently the lectionary prescribed the story of David and Bathsheba from Second Samuel as the first lesson. I decided to preach on David's adultery and its consequences. In my sermon I planned to focus mainly on how David had transgressed God's plan for his life through his lust.

The reader that Sunday happened to be a much beloved grandmother in the congregation. She read through the story aloud with beautiful emphasis and clarity. Yet when she came to the prophet Nathan's reproof of David, she read, "The child that is born to you shall die" (2 Sam. 12:14) with the pathos, pity, and sensitivity that only a grandmother can bring to such a story. We were all moved.

When I read Nathan's rebuke of David as I prepared my sermon the week before, all I heard were the fire-breathing threats of a harsh prophet. But what if Nathan, empathetic with David's plight, said those words as this grandmother said them—in regret, pity, and sorrow?

A whole new dimension of the story was opened to me because of this woman's sensitive oral interpretation of the Bible.

Remember that this oral reading was the way that the Bible was intended to be heard. If you don't get something out of every lesson which is read, don't worry. One justification for reading three lessons every Sunday is that we are thereby enriching our services with more scripture. One day the epistle may speak to you when the gospel doesn't. In listening, be patient. Sometimes a word comes to us, sometimes it doesn't. Remember, this is the church's book, the church's word. The test of scripture is not whether it is personally edifying to you but whether it is edifying to the church as a whole.

It is no easy task for you or me, for the entire church, to see things differently by hearing faithfully. We have ways of subconsciously filtering out that which is unpleasant or painful or too challenging. We hear what we want to hear. Therefore, before the scriptures are opened, Jane has led us in a Prayer for Illumination. We have prayed for the gift of the Holy Spirit to enable us joyfully to receive the gift of scripture. In so doing we admit that hearing is something of a miracle.

In today's world, with the cacophony of conflicting voices and claims, it is a wonder that any of us is able to hear. With the honking of horns and the ever present drone of the television, the car radio, and the home stereo sometimes the silence in our souls is deafening. The words of scripture are ancient, sometimes confusing, strange words. So it is no wonder that sometimes when they are read, we listen, but we do not hear.

But sometimes, often when you least expect it, often when you least want it, you are given the gift. You hear. To the very depths of your soul, you hear. The ancient words become your word. In hearing, your life is swept up into the ancient dialogue between a people who dare to listen and a God who refuses to be silent. The story becomes your story, and in response to the claim that scripture is "the Word of God," you are able to say, "Thanks be to God."

5.

Sermon

Is there any word from the Lord?

[Jesus] closed the book, and gave it back to the attendant, and sat down; and the eyes of all in the synagogue were fixed on him. And he began to say to them, "Today this scripture has been fulfilled in your hearing."

—Luke 4:20-21

After the reading of scripture, the congregation settles itself, preparing for the sermon. One receives the distinct impression that this is the worship activity for which most of the worshipers have been waiting. There is the feeling, as the congregation becomes hushed and attentive, that this is a key event on this Sunday morning. In fact, for centuries the sermon has been the main event in Protestant worship. We Protestants have fancied ourselves as "people of the word." The scripture read and interpreted has been the mainstay of our worship.

In recent years we have learned the limits of this point of view. Too often our worship is dry, dull, verbose, more like a lecture in a school, than the praise of God. Church isn't school. Of course, there is a certain amount of information to be mastered by Christians. But the main mastery this faith requires is discipleship, a way of life, not a philosophy of life. To be a Christian is to be someone who is part of a family, in a relationship to Christ.

Sometimes preaching misguides us into thinking that being a Christian is mostly a matter of knowing about Jesus rather than a matter of following Jesus. A sermon is experienced by the people in the pews as a basically passive endeavor: one person speaks and the others sit quietly and listen. No wonder so many become confused into thinking that discipleship is a passive affair.

Thus people sometimes speak of church as a filling station. They say that they come empty in order to listen to the sermon and become filled so that they have the strength to make it through another week. This analogy is problematic because it is so passive. It doesn't require anything of the recipients. It supposes that the preacher's job is to fill us up and the congregation's job is to sit back and be filled.

The relationship between the people of God and scripture is a good deal more involved than the filling station analogy would have us believe. Discipleship is not simply listening but also doing. Jesus not only preached the Good News; he enacted it in deeds of love and mercy. This is all to say that, if a person's only image of Sunday morning worship is "going to preaching," then that person has missed a great deal of Christian worship.

The Function of Preaching

And yet, the sermon is, if not the whole point of

Sunday morning, at least a major point of our worship. Years ago, people sometimes spoke of the praying, singing, and acting which preceded the sermon as "preliminaries." This implied that everything we did in worship was a mere warmup for the preaching. Our orders of worship were constructed so that everything led up to the sermon, and after the sermon we stood, sang a hymn, and went home to dinner. Once again, a very passive view of Christianity was promoted by this pattern.

Yet it is true that our singing, our confession and pardon, our reading of scripture has now led us to the sermon. We have gathered ourselves, been honest with ourselves, and focused ourselves so that we might now hear what the scriptures say to us. As we noted in the last chapter, the scriptures speak to us whether a preacher speaks on them or not. But there is something ancient and holy about someone from within the community speaking from the scriptures to God's people about God's will for their lives.

So much that we have done in today's service has a timeless, eternal quality about it. Here in the sanctuary, things move in slow, deliberate, orderly progression. Old hymns are sung whose melodies and rhythms have an ancient, classic sound about them. Many of the words of the hymns, prayers, and scripture are archaic phrases which people do not use today. And, as we have said, this tradition and traditionalism is an important aspect of the church's worship.

But now, as your pastor rises to preach, all of our praying, singing, and reading begins to hit home. The ancient liturgy has set us in an eternal context.

The sermon places us in the middle of the now. The scripture speaks of a world as real and as ancient as the most ancient stories of humanity. The sermon arises out of today's newspaper headlines, conversations with friends yesterday at work, arguments at tonight's church board meeting.

Without the sermon, there is always the danger that our liturgy might degenerate into an escape, a fantasy trip out of the cares of this world into some never-never land where pain is not really pain, decisions are not really difficult, and life floats above any cares or problems. Without this contemporary word, this present testimony to the faith, we might all simply gather, pat one another on the back, smile, sail off into our dreams, and then go back home no different than when we came.

The sermon is our primary protection against such infidelity. Christian worship, like Jewish worship, has a decidedly ethical bent to it. It makes a difference what happens when we leave this sanctuary. The test of our worship becomes our fidelity to the call to follow Jesus, not simply our success in admiring Jesus. The sermon is a necessary part of that call to discipleship in the here and now.

You can feel the hush settle over the congregation, a hush of expectancy, a hush of hopefulness. They are silent and attentive because they are hungry for a word. They are hushed at the holiness of one human being standing to testify to something which she has heard. Hush. Listen for a word. In a world of television hucksters and the talking heads which urge you to vote, give, buy, sell, enjoy, it is easy to forget the simple, stunning beauty of one human being, standing up before fellow human beings, clearing her throat, and daring to speak.

This moment is intimate. Will there be a word from the Lord? Will that word come to you, strike you where you live, get hold of your life? Will you hear your name called, called with such clarity and conviction that you can only say, Yes, here am I. Send me?

It has happened to you before, on other Sundays when you settled comfortably in the pew, not particularly expecting a word, just listening to the preacher talk—and then you bolted upright, felt something all the way to the tips of your toes, startled to hear your name called, surprised by the word of God. Don't listen now, don't pray the Prayer for Illumination, if you don't want to risk that sort of meeting.

The Risk of Good Preaching

Perhaps it occurs to you, as your preacher begins to speak, how odd this act of preaching is. Your pastor is a good speaker, but she is no entertainer. In a world saturated by the flashing images of television, where we are bombarded constantly with sight and sound, how restrained, how dull is this one standing here before us in robe, speaking with slightly hoarse voice.

No wonder that many have predicted the demise of preaching. Preaching has been castigated as authoritarian, dull, one-way communication which can't compete with the flashiness of the professionals on television.

This is no grinning, smooth, professional who confronts you now. This is your pastor; the one who cannot devote her whole week to a contrived, slick, theatrical production, because she is too busy visiting the sick in the hospital, spending time listening to your problems, teaching in the confirmation class, and administering your congregation. In a way, that's just the point. That's why everyone is expecting to hear something now.

When your pastor speaks, this is not a visiting celebrity come here to unload a pearl or two upon a gathering of strangers. This is your pastor, the one who makes her home here, in your town, with you people. Chances are, she will not sail off into unreality in her sermon, because she lives here, in this very real, sometimes very painful world with the rest of you. Any word that comes into today's sermon will be a word which has been forged on the same real-life anvil on which you must forge whatever revelation you receive. There may be speakers whom you are able to dismiss because they have their head in the clouds, because they don't know what it's like to be here, but you can't dispose of this speaker that easily. Therefore you listen.

Preaching continues to be the lifeblood of the church, continues to be the main expectation of laity for their pastor, because we know that here is the source of our life. Yet, let's be honest, many sermons which you hear, even the ones delivered by your pastor, are not all that great. Why?

Pastors have become the victims of rapidly expanding lay expectations. A couple of generations ago, a pastor was expected to be a preacher and a pastor. Today he or she is a counselor, church administrator, teacher, priest, preacher, pastor. In the round of visitation, administration, and counseling many pastors find that they have too little time for the demands of sermon preparation.

Because preaching is difficult and demanding, some pastors are tempted to let other pastoral duties crowd out what time they might have for preaching. The production of a minimum of fifty-two sermons per year, year after year, is quite a task. Sermons can be kept fresh and interesting only by continual reading and study on the part of the pastor. It's easier to visit the sick, fill out forms, work with the youth than to carve out study time.

Sermons are exercises in faith. Few human activities are as demanding. Every time a preacher stands to speak, his or her inner soul is laid bare before the hearers. Preachers sometimes joke about the butterflies they feel in the pit of their stomachs before they speak. But it is no joke to stand and testify to the faith, the faith that you personally have experienced or hope to experience. In sermons my own faith is laid on the line.

Biblical preaching requires a wide array of skills which are not easily gained. Not only must a preacher have a thorough grasp of this ancient, often confusing book, but he or she must also be able to put the fruits of biblical study into terms which the laity can grasp, must relate the Bible to everyday life. Too often preachers succeed at one aspect of preaching but not the other. Their biblical study is accurate but incomprehensible to the person in the pew. Or their sermons are lively, relevant, engaging, but woefully unbiblical.

Finally, and perhaps most importantly, preaching is difficult because of the very nature of the gospel itself. Jesus preached away more people than he reached. His message is full of tough, difficult sayings—not so difficult to understand but extremely difficult to accept! Have pity on the poor preacher who must say unpleasant things to people he or she has come to love. There is a sense in which the laity may not want "good preaching" as much as they think they do!

A Listener's Guide to Preaching

Even though we often think of preaching as a one-way street—someone talking to people who passively sit and listen—all preaching is dialogical. Like all communication, it takes at least two to preach. Congregations need to be reminded that sometimes preaching in their church is poor because they have put too little into it.

One of the beautiful things about preaching within the congregation, as opposed to preaching on the radio or television, is that this is your pastor, the person who lives where you live. This isn't a religious address which is delivered to all Americans in general. This is the word for the folk at your church, born out of the intersection between the pastor's Bible study and the pastor's care of the congregation. So there is a sense in which you have been helping your pastor to write the sermon all week long. The word you hear is the word which your pastor is convinced needs to be said within this congregation which stands under the word of God.

We could get more out of preaching if we put more into it. How can we put more into it?

Earlier I spoke of the sermon as an essentially passive activity. But it need not be. There is passive listening in which we sit back and dare the speaker to penetrate our apathy and our boredom. There is also active listening in which we work with the speaker to enable the speaker's words to penetrate our lives.

Have you prepared yourself to hear the sermon? In the last chapter we mentioned the value of preaching from the Common Lectionary. If your pastor does so, or if your pastor publicizes his or her sermon texts in advance, study them at home before you come to church. Prepare yourself by asking yourself questions about the proposed topic of the sermon before you hear it. Assume that your preacher has something that you need to hear. Actively listen for that word while you are listening to the sermon. Prepare yourself to be surprised, to think about things in a new way, to hear something which you may not immediately comprehend or find useful.

Your church could tell your pastor that you expect good preaching, that you deserve good preaching, and that you are willing to provide the time, study, and training necessary for good preaching. Have you encouraged or allowed your pastor to crowd his or her schedule with activities which could be done as well by qualified laypersons? Do you support an active program of continuing education, recreation, and refreshment for your pastor?

Praise your preacher when you feel that he or she has struggled to preach well. Preaching is a creative activity. Sometimes a sermon goes flat not because the preacher did not work on the sermon but because it failed to "happen" in the moment of delivery. A sermon, as we have said, is a joint undertaking of preacher and congregation. A sermon is a gift of the Holy Spirit. Sometimes this all comes together and it is wonderful; sometimes it doesn't, and the sermon falls upon deaf ears. Whenever a preacher tries to be creative and risks a sermon beyond the conventional three points and a closing poem, there is always the possibility that the sermon may fail. Understand that risk and support your preacher in his or her creativity.

Let your preacher know that you are not hostile when confronted by controversial subjects in sermons. One reason that so many sermons are boring and inconsequential is that preachers become shell-shocked by congregational criticism and anger when the preacher "mixes religion and politics" or tackles "controversial" subjects. Eventually, the preacher wears down and sticks to the safe confines of thoroughly conventional and acceptable subjects. Support your preacher's freedom and responsibility to preach the word—whether that word offends or pleases. Realize the courage it takes to speak an unpopular word to people whom one loves.

That does not mean that you must agree with everything that is said in a sermon. Most preachers take it as a great compliment when someone has listened so well to their sermon that a person wants to discuss some issue further. Most good preaching begins when someone says, "I was troubled by your idea on capital punishment. Can we talk about this over coffee next week?" In these moments preaching expands from a one-way street to true dialogue, and the church becomes the community of moral discourse that it is meant to be.

All of this is to say that many congregations get poor preaching—and deserve it!

So, as you listen to your pastor's sermon, it occurs to you that, even though you are sitting quietly in the pew, this act of worship is not as passive as you once thought it to be. It does take more than one to preach the gospel. Like any other act of worship, the sermon is also an activity, an active engagement of your powers of praise and adoration of God. Earlier in the service, you have joined in the prayers, songs, speaking, and action of the church in order to come close to God. Now, in the sermon, you are coming close to God through the word. Here is yet another act of worship, another attempt to let God be God, to let the Holy Spirit work its way with your life.

6.

Creed

*Let us stand and affirm
what we believe.*

When your son asks you in time to come,
"What is the meaning of the testimonies and
the statutes and the ordinances which the
Lord our God has commanded you?" then you
shall say to your son, "We were Pharaoh's
slaves in Egypt; and the Lord brought us out of
Egypt with a mighty hand; and the Lord
showed signs and wonders."

—Deuteronomy 6:20-22

The sermon ends and
the congregation moves
into the part of the service which is called, "Response
to the Word." From here on everything which happens is response to what you have heard. You have
heard the word read (in scripture), heard the word
proclaimed (in the sermon), now it's your turn to
stand and affirm the word in the creed.

"Let us rise and affirm our faith," says your pastor.
All rise and repeat the ancient, familiar words of
the Apostles' Creed, "I believe in God the Father

almighty, creator of heaven and earth. I believe in Jesus Christ, his only Son, our Lord."

I Believe

Credo, "I believe." These are stirring, courageous words. In modern conversation, "I believe" often means "I suppose" or "I am not certain." For Paul, as well as in the tradition of the church, "I believe" means more—"I commit myself to this." In today's cautious, tentative, uncertain world, we would be more biblically accurate to say, "I wholly believe."

When Fidel Castro led Cuba through a Marxist revolution, pressure was put upon the churches and individual Christians to forsake their faith. There were few outright persecutions, but there were many not-so-subtle hints that Christianity would be unpopular in the new Cuba. Overnight, bumper stickers began appearing on many automobiles in Havanna which read, *Credo in Deo, Credo in Christo*. I believe in God, I believe in Christ. When we say "I believe," we are saying it in much the same way as those risky, courageous Cuban bumper stickers.

We live in an age of action and experience. You often hear people say, "It's not so important what you believe as long as you act right," or "Actions speak louder than words."

Yet, every Sunday, when you come to this point in the service and stand and say, "I believe . . ." you affirm that what we believe does make a big difference. Right beliefs can lead to right action. All beliefs are not equally true, no matter how sincerely someone believes them. The most dastardly acts of history were committed by "sincere" people who sincerely believed that their actions were righteous.

Women were tried and convicted of witchcraft in Salem. Doubters were burned at the stake in the Inquisition. Little children were sent to the gas chambers at Dachau. Those who committed these deeds were wrong, dead wrong, to believe what they believed.

In saying "I believe" we are also challenging the modern notion that I can only affirm what has personally happened to me. Religion is an intensely personal, private, emotional, experiential matter; but religion is also a social, corporate, communal, historical matter as well. You and I build our faith on a foundation laid by others who have believed before us. We don't have to "reinvent the wheel" in our faith. Rather than being heirs to a glorious heritage of faith, many of us moderns have become (in the words of G. K. Chesterton) slaves to "the arrogant oligarchy of those who happen to be walking about."

In the introduction to the Service of Evensong at Coventry Cathedral, we read, "You are entering a conversation which began long before you were born and shall continue long after you are dead." That's the Creed. It is a shorthand statement of the traditional perimeters of the faith. It is also a reminder that what we believe does make a difference.

Creeds grew in the church's first five centuries as a means of objectifying the church's experience of the risen Christ. If that experience is to be passed on from generation to generation, it must be more than the personal, subjective property of the first disciples. Tradition comes from the Latin word *tradere*, literally "to hand over." The Creed is what one generation of believers hands over to the next.

Proclaiming the Mighty Acts of God

The deeds of God in Christ bring the church into being. The church then continually recites these deeds as a means of telling the world and retelling ourselves what has happened to us in Christ. Creeds are not primarily a way to "check out" the beliefs of individual members, official tests of orthodoxy or heresy, though creeds have been used in this way from time to time in the past. The Creed is the Church's earnest, continual attempt to witness to the facts. A creed is thus a hymn, a joyous shout because of what has happened.

The earliest creeds are found in the Hebrew scriptures. The faith of Israel is founded not upon personal feelings or inner yearnings toward God but rather God's acts toward Israel. A Jew is someone who tells the story of what God has done. Thus, the passover is celebrated by reciting a creed: "When your children say to you, 'What do you mean by this service?' You shall say, 'It is the sacrifice of the Lord's passover, for he passed over the houses of the people of Israel in Egypt, when he slew the Egyptians but spared our houses'" (Exod. 12:26-27).

Israel's worship is, in great part, the fulfillment of the psalmist's claim that "one generation shall laud thy works to another, and shall declare thy mighty acts" (Psalm 145:4).

The earliest New Testament creed was probably the simple, "Jesus Christ is Lord," a creed which people repeated as they were baptized. Soon this simple creed took the trinitarian shape of the Apostles' Creed. This creed was a response to the three questions at baptism.

Do you believe in God the Father?

I believe in God, the Father almighty, creator of heaven and earth.

Do you believe in Jesus Christ?

I believe in Jesus Christ, his only Son, our Lord.
He was conceived by the power of the Holy Spirit
    and born of the Virgin Mary.
He suffered under Pontius Pilate,
    was crucified, died, and was buried.
He descended to the dead.
On the third day he rose again.
He ascended into heaven,
    and is seated at the right hand of the Father.
He will come again
    to judge the living and the dead.

Do you believe in the Holy Spirit?

I believe in the Holy Spirit,
    the holy catholic Church,
    the communion of saints,
    the forgiveness of sins,
    the resurrection of the body,
    and the life everlasting.

Fortunately, new liturgies for baptism put this responsive creed back in its proper place at baptism. That's why the Creed appears at this point in the Sunday service, at the same point when baptism occurs, if there is to be one. Because the Apostles' Creed is the baptismal creed, everytime we recite it, we are renewing our baptism, telling again the story which led to our baptism and our salvation by God in Christ. We also use other creeds in our worship—the Nicene Creed or the modern creed of the United Church of Canada, for example.

The church is not merely the place where pious feelings are promoted, not even the place where good deeds are encouraged. First, the church is the place where the acts of God are proclaimed. Here the story is told, Sunday after Sunday. Because of God's actions, we re-act and en-act, responding in word and deed to what has happened. The agenda of the church is prescribed by what God has done and will do in the world, not by what the church may feel is practical and permissible. Our job is to tell the story. The Creed is the story. It is our enactment of the psalmist's cry, "All thy works shall give thanks to thee, O Lord, and all thy saints shall bless thee" (Psalm 145:10).

An early baptismal sermon declares that Christians have been saved, washed, adopted, empowered by God for no more important reason than to proclaim to the world the marvelous work of God: "But you are a chosen race, a royal priesthood, a holy nation, God's own people, that you may declare the wonderful deeds of him who called you out of darkness into his marvelous light" (1 Pet. 2:9).

The Function of the Creed

Yet, as you say the Creed, repeating these familiar words learned by heart, a thought troubles you: "What if I'm really not sure about all this? The virgin birth? The resurrection? Do I *really* believe what I am saying?"

Some Sundays you stand confidently and say these words. You do indeed believe. But, to be honest,

there are Sundays when you are not so sure. These words of the Creed sound foreign, remote from you and your innermost thoughts. On these Sundays, it might be more accurate for you to say, "I (wish I could) believe" in the "forgiveness of sins, the resurrection of the body, and the life everlasting."

How can you stand and affirm the Creed without lying? Are there no limits to how much the church asks you to swallow? Might it be more honest of you simply to remain seated during the Creed, keep silent, and pass to someone else who is more convinced until you can say for sure what you believe?

We need to be clear about what the church is asking you to do in the Creed. Don't be confused by the opening phrase, "I believe." In saying "I believe" you are, of course, affirming what is true for you. "What is true" is being defined by the Creed as the faith of the church. You cannot be affirming what you have personally experienced when you say you believe in the virgin birth of Christ. Nor can you be saying that you believe this on the basis of scientific research or objective "proof"—as we usually define proof. You are not even saying that you believe because "recent surveys show that 99 percent of all Americans agree."

You are saying that you believe that the testimony of the apostles, the word of the witnesses, the tradition of the church is true. It is fair for you to have doubts about various aspects of the Creed—who doesn't sometimes wonder how, when, or why certain strange claims really happened? But it is not fair for you to say that because you have not personally seen these things, or that you were not personally present when they occurred, that you cannot believe.

Only the most arrogantly ignorant could demand such proof.

When I board a jet for a flight, I am saying, in effect, "I believe this plane will fly." I do so without the slightest understanding of how it flies or why. I know nothing of aerodynamics or jet propulsion. All I know is that I have successfully flown before on jets. I trust, even though I have no real personal experience or proof that my trust is based upon fact. I trust in spite of my lack of proof.

The belief you are affirming in the Creed is the church's belief. Any proof you seek must finally be in the pudding which is the church. Either here, at your church, in worship, fellowship, and service, you have experienced the resurrection, the lordship of Christ, and the reign of God, or little the church can say will help defend the claims of the Creed.

In a sense, when you say "I believe," you are often saying that you, as an individual Christian, are on your way to believing what the church believes. Don't be troubled by individual reservations or doubts. Certainty may come in time. Lots of things that seemed absurd or irrelevant to me at age seventeen seem much more likely now that I am nearly forty.

Besides, even if one hundred percent certainty doesn't come, in affirming the faith of the church you have affirmed what is true. You have not been so presumptuous as to assume that the truth of a doctrine rises or falls on your personal acceptance. If the reality of jet flight rested upon my personal understanding or belief in the laws of aerodynamics, we would all be riding rather than flying. There is an objectivity to truth which transcends my subjective limitations.

One might say that you should recite the Creed *especially* when you have difficulty believing it. If you do not feel that sin is forgiven, that may be your problem, not God's. Keep telling yourself, let the church keep telling you, "I believe in the forgiveness of sins." Eventually, it may all come home to you. What is true may become true for *you*.

As the church's Creed, sometimes when you believe and say it, you are saying it for the person who is next to you in the pew, the person who may be doubting and empty now. In saying the Creed, in witnessing to that person's unbelief, you are, in matters of belief, doing unto others as you would have them do unto you.

In a world full of vengeance, it isn't easy to believe in forgiveness. In a nuclear-proliferated universe where chaos threatens, it isn't easy to stand and say, with a clear voice, "I believe in God the Father almighty," and really believe that someone is in charge. This is all the more reason that the church must repeat these words, say them aloud and with courage until we come to believe that which, on so many Sundays, we wish we could believe.

Sometimes love comes naturally and easily to us. But in much of life, we make love in order to fall in love. We make believe in order to believe.

This is not to say that anyone can believe anything he or she wants, blissfully repeating the Creed, and do so with integrity. What we believe does make a difference. This is the faith of the church, the tradition we have received from the saints before us, a conversation with God which began long before we were born and shall continue long after we are dead. In repeating these words, we honor that tradition and demonstrate our determination to be open to God's gifts, no matter what the cost. Therefore we repeat these words seriously, with a sense of awe, even fear, knowing that, if they are true, true for us, for all eternity, then we may now have some painful changing to do.

What we believe *does* make a difference.

7

Intercession
Let us pray.

Your Father knows what you need before you ask him. Pray then like this.

—*Matthew 6:8-9*

Your pastor moves to the middle of the chancel. She now leads the congregation in the Prayer for Others, the Intercession: "Let us pray that the world may live in peace, and that the church may achieve unity, fulfilling its service here and everywhere."

And the people respond, "This is our prayer."

You note that this prayer comes after the sermon. It is as if all our preaching, singing, confessing, have gathered us for this act of worship. Formerly, we sometimes had the "Pastoral Prayer" which usually came earlier in the service, well before the sermon. Too often the Pastoral Prayer was just that, a personal prayer of the pastor to which the congregation listened. It occurred too early, before we were ready, before we knew for what to pray. Now, having heard the word, we are ready.

Without the word we might not know how to pray.

"Teach us to pray" was one of the few things the disciples asked of Jesus. He gave them a model for prayer, saying, "Our Father who art in heaven . . . . " Tertullian calls the Lord's Prayer "an epitome of the whole gospel."

Today, as we come to this time of intercession in the service, we, like those disciples before us, have come to Jesus asking, "Teach us to pray." We have been instructed by the word. The word helps us to discern between true and false prayer, between praying as a pagan and praying as a Christian. It tells us what it means to pray "in Jesus' name," in the spirit of our Lord. That's why the Prayer of Intercession comes here.

The prayer also comes here, close to the offering, because, having heard the word, this is our time to offer ourselves to the God who has offered himself to us. We are not simply telling God what we want, rather, we are now placing our wants within the context of God's will for the world. As Paul says, "We do not know how to pray as we ought" (Rom. 8:26). Presumably, prayer, truly Christian prayer, is not something which comes naturally. Knowing that God's will may be different from ours, we begin and end this prayer as Jesus taught us: Nevertheless, not my will, but thine be done.

In praying for others and in making intercession for the needs of the world, we walk along a treacherous terrain. This moment when we are so bold as to ask God to do something to make our lives and our world better is a risky endeavor. Unless intercession comes after praise, confession, the word, there is great danger that we will be wrong in what we ask. As Paul noted, the Holy Spirit teaches us to pray. Presumably, in our time of worship, some of our smothering self-concern has been lifted. We have been moved from self-protection and narrow personal desires and focused upon something, someone greater than ourselves.

Throughout this whole service of worship, we have been attempting to love God, to take God's desires a little more seriously and our desires a little less so. All of this has been in the service of, in the words of the old hymn, "More love to thee, O Christ, more love to thee!"

Now, in asking God for good, we are once again focusing upon ourselves and how we fit into God's kingdom, offering ourselves in service of the petition that "thy kingdom come, thy will be done, on earth as it is in heaven."

Teach Us to Pray

Prayer is a problem for many modern people. What are we doing here? What are we supposed to ask for? What to say?

For some, prayer has become little more than auto-suggestion, self-therapy. In their view, prayer is mainly of value in helping us to get our heads straight about what we ought to want and do. Prayer is a time for quiet meditation so that we might enter ever more deeply into our own egos.

Note how many prayers are addressed to ourselves, rather than God. "Make us ever more mindful," we say. Our prayers become thinly disguised preaching, practical atheism in which God doesn't really matter because we are only talking to ourselves. This makes prayer seem silly, pointless.

As John Wesley once said, "The end of your pray-

ing is not to inform God, as though he knew not your wants already, but rather to inform yourselves." Wesley's suggestion is dangerous. Is God there or not? That may not have been a question for Wesley, but it is for us. Is there anyone "out there" who hears and who cares? This frightening, fundamental question is at the heart of this time of prayer. Everything depends upon the answer. It will not do to fudge on this one and say things like, "Prayer is mainly of value in putting us in the right frame of mind to solve the problems which beset us." Either we are speaking to a God who acts, or we are merely prattling on to ourselves.

Yet in asking God for things, we have said, "Thy will be done on earth as it is in heaven." Prayer is conversation with God not magic. Prayer is not some magical formula through which we hope to entice an apathetic God to act in a way which pleases us. Our prayer is the worshipful recognition that God is continually acting in the world and the signifying of our desire to be part of that activity. God will be working for good in the world, for order out of chaos, for justice and peace, whether we do or not.

If we really want peace, food, justice, then we should resort not to prayer but to action to change these situations. If these problems cannot be altered, then we must endure the frustration and disappointment and find a way of living without despair.

In prayer we ask for what God can and will do. But we also, in prayer, acknowledge, "Thy will be done," realizing what God does not do. There are many things we ask God to do—feed the hungry, make peace, work reconciliation—which we are unwilling to do because of the sacrifice and struggle, the conversion and suffering it might cause us. Yet there are things which God, for some reason, cannot or will not do. Why? We usually do not understand why we pray for badly needed rain and get none or ask for a tumor to be healed and it becomes worse. Prayer does not usually answer the Why? But our prayer can give us the faith to live in spite of the lack of answers. And, for the Christian, that faith is considered a good deal more valuable even than answers.

Curiously, even as modern humanity has been successful at solving so many of its problems with more research, better hygiene, advances in technology, we are impressed with how seemingly insoluble are many problems. Ecological crisis, shortage of natural resources, overpopulation, war, economic decline, nuclear proliferation—many despair that we have the capacity to solve these big issues.

Perhaps because we have succeeded in solving some age-old human dilemmas, we assume that we can eradicate every evil and cure every ill. Likewise, because God is good and generous in so many areas of life, we assume that God must do all that our hearts desire.

It is natural, in a world where we get most of what we want, with pushbutton speed, that we should assume that prayer is a technique for getting what we want.

No. For us now, in worship, joining our voices in intercession for the world, prayer is a means of getting what God wants.

A woman lay in a hospital bed, body inflamed by the spread of cancer. Day after day we prayed for healing. Each day I could see her silent disappointment that she was not being healed.

Then one day she said, "Today let's not pray that I'll be healed. God knows that I hate this illness. God knows I want to be healed. Let's pray that, whether I'm healed or not, I'll feel close to God because even if I'm not healed, especially if I'm not healed, that's what I really want—God."

She reminded me that, when all is said and done, we want not simply peace, justice, health, bread. We want God. We pray that God's will be done on earth as it is in heaven. In one sense this means that we want God as present to us on earth as God is present in heaven. Thus we must not be confused into thinking that now, in prayer, we have stopped worshiping and have started asking God to do things for us. We are continuing to lay ourselves open to the presence of God, no matter what.

In prayer we are allying ourselves with that will, making our desires more congruent with God's desires. We don't simply wish that the poor should be fed, but that we should be participants in God's active love for the poor. We open ourselves up to new possibilities for participating in the reign of God. So our prayer is education in desire, voicing our desires, placing them next to the desires of God as expressed in word and sacrament.

That the leaders of this nation and of the world may govern with justice and mercy:
This is our prayer.

That those who suffer disease or poverty or loneliness or grief may be healed and comforted; that those who are oppressed or persecuted may be

strengthened and delivered:
This is our prayer.

That those whom we have known and loved and who have died in the faith may be a glorious memory to us and a source of renewed fellowship with all the saints:
This is our prayer, through Jesus Christ our Lord. Amen.
—From *The Sacrament of the Lord's Supper,
An Alternate Text, 1972*

It is proper to be specific here, to get down to concrete particulars of what our hearts desire, to say our petitions aloud, in public, as you are doing now. In so doing, we bring these wants to the light of truth. Now, in public, our wants are judged, purified, motivated. To pray "in Jesus' name" means to pray as he prayed in Gethsemane, ready to submit to the will of God, ready to be part of the coming kingdom, even if its advent means our suffering.

The church which prays for healing is usually the one which is willing to change the bandages, empty the bedpans, keep the night vigils. In our social concern and work for justice we are only doing what we asked for in prayer. Our work is an extension of our prayer, not a substitute for it, and vice versa. As Rabbi Abraham Joshua Heschel described the freedom march at Selma, Alabama: "For many of us the march from Selma to Montgomery was both protest and prayer. Legs are not lips, and walking is not kneeling. And yet our legs uttered songs. Even without words, our march was worship. I felt my legs were praying."

To pray "in Jesus' name" means to position ourselves to look at life as he did, to stand not above the poor, the sick, the oppressed, and the lonely but beside them. Gradually, if we keep at it, as the scriptures urge us to be persistent, we find that the desires we wanted to lift up to God have been converted. "Give me, give me," sometimes becomes "Make me, make me." Prayer changes things—even us!

We are not praying to just any god. We bow before the God of Abraham and Sarah, the God to whom Mary said "I am the handmaid of the Lord," and to whom Jesus said, "Thy will be done." Our prayers are faithful and possible only as they relate to the desires of this God.

8.

The Lord's Supper

Let us offer ourselves and our gifts to God.

They devoted themselves to the apostles' teaching and fellowship, to the breaking of bread and the prayers. *—Acts 2:42*

Two people pass one another on the sidewalk. Their eyes meet. Then they reach out to one another, they may embrace or shake hands. What you are witnessing is a daily ritual of meeting. By such rituals we enact those moments in life which are too deep for words; through gesture and sign we enact who we are and want to be. How dull, detached, and isolated our lives would be without these everyday rituals of greeting and meeting.

Now, having heard the word and having said the prayers, your pastor invites you to make peace. This "passing of the peace" is not always well received in every congregation. You have found that it sometimes takes some effort before it becomes part of you. At this point, people are invited to stand and embrace one another, often speaking such words as "The peace of God be with you," or a simple "Peace," or whatever feels natural to you.

125

The Peace is an ancient Christian greeting of peace and reconciliation. It arises from Jesus' instruction: "So if you are offering your gift at the altar, and there remember that your brother [or sister] has something against you, leave your gift there before the altar and go; first be reconciled to your brother [or sister], and then come and offer your gift" (Matt. 5:23-24).

In other words, Jesus tells us that it is wrong to presume to offer our gifts of prayer, money, bread, wine, and service to God when we have not first offered our service to one another in the Peace. Christian worship is made into a mockery when we gather, sing hymns, smile, and think warm, religious thoughts while we hold grudges, old hurts, and past wrongs against our brothers and sisters. The Peace offers us the opportunity to be reconciled to one another even as we seek to be reconciled to God.

Yet sometimes, in some segments of our culture, we are not comfortable with such gestures. The simple shaking of hands is usually accepted, but many of us are uncomfortable with anything beyond that, particularly in church! In church we come and sit in rows of pews, carefully separated from one another as if we were fearful of close contact.

The Peace is a vehicle whereby we are given the opportunity to meet, a means of doing what we might like to do but may not have the courage to do. You didn't like doing the Peace at first. You felt uncomfortable turning to a stranger next to you in the pew, embracing and saying, "The peace of God be with you." It seemed contrived, forced, unnatural. Yet, with your pastor's encouragement and example, you kept at it. It has become more natural for you, less forced.

When you think about it, that's what the church has tried to do for you, not only in this act of worship called the Peace, but in all of the activities and worship of the church—enable you to be reconciled, encourage you to reach out to God and to your brothers and sisters. You have found that in daring to embrace a stranger you transform a stranger from an alien into a friend.

Here, in church, the Peace, however it is done, reminds you that the church which stands under the gospel of Christ and gathers at his table, regards no one as a stranger and estranged. Here, at the Lord's table, we see a vision of peace which only the love of God brings, a peace so compelling that it transforms even strangers like us into a family.

After the prayers and the Peace, your pastor stands before the congregation and says, "Let us offer ourselves and our gifts to God."

Frankly, you are not too sure about this act of worship. Part of you wonders if the offering is an intrusion in the service, a break in what has, up to this point, been inspiring. Perhaps it would be better if our church followed the custom of the old Church of England and simply put a collection plate in the rear of the church, near the doors, so that people could put in their money upon entering or leaving the building. Somehow, after the beautiful music, the moving sermon, the prayers, this bustle of ushers and passing of plates, this jingling of money seems out of place.

Of course, you know that the church needs money to operate. Most of the church's causes receive your wholehearted support. But couldn't they find a more appropriate time of collection than now?

Let Us Offer Ourselves and Our Gifts

You remember a time when the offering occurred earlier in the service, well before the sermon. Why has it been put here? You are becoming more accustomed to having it here, but you remember a time when it was your church's custom to have all of these "preliminaries" earlier. Then everyone settled down to hear the sermon. After the sermon everyone stood, sang a hymn, and departed. What was wrong with that?

Historically, the offering was the bridge between the first part of the service, the Service of the Word, and the second part, the Service of the Table. For fifteen hundred years, up until the time of the Protestant Reformation, Christians worshiped in this general pattern. They gathered to read and listen to the word. Then they received the gifts (bread, wine, money) and moved to the table. Most of the major Protestant reformers, like Luther and Calvin, hoped to continue this practice. Unfortunately, in most Protestant churches, the Service of the Table became disjoined from the Service of the Word, and Holy Communion or the Lord's Supper was celebrated infrequently. When that happened, the offering drifted to other places in the service.

In the early church, the offering consisted of the people's gifts of bread and wine for the holy meal. In the introduction to this book we read Justin Martyr's account of an early Christian service. Justin describes this collection of the communion elements. After the service, leftovers were taken to "the orphans and the widows, and those who are needy because of sickness or other cause, and the captives, and the strangers who sojourn amongst us."

In this Sunday's service, the offering has been restored to its position just before we come to the Lord's table. But who cares if the offering was in this position two hundred years ago? We live in the age of plastic money, the charge card, computerized banking, and revolving credit. Couldn't the church find a more efficient, less intrusive way of collecting its due?

Pay attention as the plate is being passed down the pew, as people place their gifts in it, pay attention as the Jones family comes forward when the offering is received, bringing the loaf of bread and the pitcher of wine for Holy Communion, for something very important is happening here. Occurring here, as a bridge between the word spoken in the sermon and the word enacted at the table, the offering is a significant statement of faith. How so?

The persistent danger of our Sunday worship, the sacrilege against which we must be eternally vigilant, is the tendency to divorce Sunday worship from daily life. It is the danger that all our hymns, our anthems, our soft organ voluntaries, our poetic preachers, our beautiful churches might somehow conspire to turn worship into an event which has nothing to do with everyday life. Unless there is some link between our worship of God and junior's spilt cereal at breakfast, the boring routine at the office, the monthly collection of bills, the cancer which will not heal, then our worship is not only irrelevant to human need but also unfaithful to the gospel of Jesus Christ.

Never think that Sunday worship is mostly a

"spiritual" affair, as we like to use the word spiritual.
Christianity is an incarnational faith, meaning "in the
body." Jesus is here as a visible, tangible sign that
God could truly love us only by coming "in the
body," by becoming incarnate in a Jewish carpenter's
son from Nazareth. There may be religions where
practice is confined to what you do in some holy
place, hermetically sealed from the stress and strain
of everyday life. There may be religions in which
things like political debate, bodily health, material
well being, and physical needs are irrelevant. Christianity is not one of those religions. Here is a Lord
who comes to us, not to take us out of this world but
to give us a way to live in this world.

Every time we receive the offering, we are giving
visible, tangible expression to the materiality of the
Christian faith. We are lifting up ordinary things like
bread, wine, and money and saying that because of
the life, teachings, death, and resurrection of Jesus,
these ordinary things take on new significance for us.
In his ministry Jesus was always taking the everyday
stuff of life—seeds, birds, flowers, coins, lepers, children—lifting them up, setting them in the context of
God's kingdom, and thereby giving them redemptive
significance. After meeting Jesus, after listening to
his stories, you can't walk by a hungry person, or lift
up a loaf of bread, or pick a flower, or gaze into the
eyes of a child quite the same way as you did before
meeting him. Ours is an incarnational faith.

How many times have you felt that your minister was forever urging you to "get out there and
do something" but never gave you anything specific
to do?

Now, in the offering, it is your chance to do something. The offering is, in a way, the test of our worship. Is this service only a time to sing a few hymns, think a few lofty thoughts, feel a few warm fuzzies, and go home to a big meal? Or is this a time to "put our money where our mouth is"? Remember how Jesus noted that our hearts are usually where our money is and vice versa.

The offering isn't an unwarranted intrusion; it is the acid test of what we are about. It yokes our faith to our jobs, our daily cares and concerns, what we shall eat, what we wear, where we live, how we vote. We shouldn't apologize or be embarrassed by this act of worship, for it is an act which typifies the peculiar Christian stance toward the world, a stance typified by the person of Jesus himself.

"I think that the main business of the church is to stick to saving souls and stay out of politics."

"I think preachers should stick with theology and avoid controversial subjects like economic, business, or political matters."

"What a person gives or doesn't give is his or her own business."

"I'm tired of churches talking about nothing but money, money, money. They should be concerned with more spiritual matters."

How we wish it were so!

In a former church of mine, we were in a board meeting debating how to conduct the church's annual stewardship campaign. The discussion was becoming heated, emotions were beginning to boil. One member said, "I get so tired of all this talk about money. I hope that we can get this kind of thing out of the way and get on to more important church business—like religion!"

I responded, "Well, what is our business? Perhaps all this talk about money is not a religious matter. But don't you find it interesting that we have been meeting all year, discussing all manner of church business without even a mild argument? Yet, when we discuss money, suddenly everyone gets very heated. I have a feeling that we may at last be discussing *the* really big concern for most of us."

The offering is the link, the necessary connection between our intentions and our deeds, our spiritual impulses and our materialistic commitments. The offering reminds us that Christian worship is an ethical affair. A Christian does in church on Sunday that which he or she does Monday through Saturday in the world, namely, to offer one's life to God. Our actions, our gifts, our deeds are our offering, our way of giving back to the God who has so graciously given to us.

On many Sundays in your church, only money is received, rather than the gifts of bread and wine. The service draws to a close with a Prayer of Thanksgiving, hymns, and benediction. This Sunday, bread and wine are brought forward now and the congregation moves toward the table.

Signs of Love

"Don't talk of love, show me!" pleads Eliza Doolittle in the Broadway musical *My Fair Lady*. Saying "I love you" is saying something wonderful. But sometimes we need more than words. We communicate with one another not only by speech but also by action, gesture, symbol, and touch. "Actions speak louder than words," we say.

God knows this. In the Bible, God not only says, "I

love you, I want you to be my people," through the
words of the Hebrew law, the sermons of the prophets, the teachings of Jesus, and the letters of Paul;
God's love is also demonstrated.

God's love is demonstrated through signs. "And
this will be a sign for you: you will find a babe
wrapped in swaddling cloths and lying in a manger"
(Luke 2:12). When we look into the manger at Bethlehem and see the babe, we see a visible, inescapably
human sign that God is acting to redeem his people.

God's love is also demonstrated through symbols.
When you go to a wedding, you see the bride and
groom exchange words of love and commitment. But
rings are also given with the explanation that "the
wedding ring is an outward and visible sign of an
inward and spiritual grace." The rings become symbols to those who wear them of the promises they
have made.

Of course, an outside observer may look at a symbol such as a flag and say, "That's only a square of
cotton cloth with some red, white, and blue dye on
it." The wedding ring is only a piece of metal. But to
those who fly the flag as a symbol of their beloved
homeland, or who wear the rings as a sign of their
promises, these powerful symbols express in a visible
and tangible way the deepest and most inexpressible
feelings in their lives. There are some human emotions that are too deep, too mysterious for mere
words. The depth of human emotion can be plumbed
only through sign, symbol, gesture, touch.

A flag, a handshake, a kiss, a cross, a wedding
ring—these are all symbols of love which express far
more than words can express. For us Christians,
Jesus himself became the supreme visible and tan-

gible symbol which expresses and reveals God's love
for us. This is the way the Gospel of John puts it:

> The Word became flesh and dwelt among us, full of
> grace and truth; we have beheld his glory, glory as of the
> only Son from the Father. . . . And from his fulness have
> we all received, grace upon grace . . . . No one has ever
> seen God; only the Son, who is in the bosom of the
> Father, he has made him known.
>
> —*John 1:14, 16, 18.*

In worship we use objects and actions to show our
love for God. We praise God by dressing in our Sunday best, by putting flowers from our garden next to
the altar, by singing for God, parading down the aisle
in a processional for God. These are our signs and
symbols of love. God also uses certain signs and
symbols, which we call sacraments, to demonstrate
his love for us. Our Creator knows that we creatures
depend upon demonstrations of divine love, so God
uses everyday things we can understand to show us
love which defies understanding. God gives us the
Christ: "In many and various ways God spoke of old
to our fathers by the prophets; but in these last days
he has spoken to us by a Son" (Heb. 1:1-2).

The Holy Meal

Throughout Jesus' ministry, meals play a central
part in his message. Thumb through any one of the
Gospels and you see Jesus at a recession of meals,
each of which reveals something significant about
this new kingdom which he proclaims. You remember the wedding at Cana where he turned the water
into wine so that the joy might continue, the meal at
the house of Levi where Jesus was criticized for eating

and drinking with outcasts, the meal where he fed
the five thousand and thus ministered to the hunger
of the multitudes, the story he told of the meal which
was celebrated in honor of the return of the prodigal
son. Here was God's messenger who did not simply
come speaking a message of divine love. This messenger became the message, he enacted words of love
by deeds of love.

Interestingly, the earliest charge against Jesus was
not "this man is a heretic and a social revolutionary."
Rather, Jesus' critics looked at his behavior and cried
that he was a "glutton and a drunkard, a friend of tax
collectors and sinners!" (Luke 7:34). Jesus refused to
accept the social and religious barriers which people
erect around the table. He broke with convention and
feasted with everyone. One memorable evening, at
the table of a ruler he said,

> "When you give a dinner or a banquet, do not invite
> your friends or your brothers or your kinsmen or rich
> neighbors, lest they also invite you in return, and you be
> repaid. But when you give a feast, invite the poor, the
> maimed, the lame, the blind, and you will be blessed,
> because they cannot repay you."
>
> —Luke 14:12-14

For Jesus, the table becomes a witness to the inclusiveness of God's kingdom, a visible enactment of
the message which he proclaimed at his first sermon
in Nazareth: "The Spirit of the Lord is upon me,
because he has anointed me to preach good news to
the poor . . . to proclaim release to the captives and
recovering of sight to the blind" (Luke 4:18).

Then Jesus told a memorable parable about a feast
(Luke 14:15-24). A man gives a great banquet and

invites all his friends and cronies. He sends his servant to proclaim, "Come; for all is now ready." But the response of those who are invited is scandalous: they make excuses. One says he has bought a field and has not seen it. Another says that he has bought five yoke of oxen and must now examine them. Another has married a wife! By this time the hearers of the story are rolling on the floor with raucous laughter. The excuses, especially when given in response to so great a feast, are ridiculous. In that part of the world, where land and livestock are purchased at a premium, it would be unthinkable that one would buy such expensive items without first examining them. And what Near Eastern male would let a little thing like a wife keep him from attending a great banquet?

The host is angered. To refuse an invitation to someone's table, especially for reasons that are frivolous, is a great insult. The master sends the servant out again, this time to the streets of the city. Who is now invited to the table? "The poor and maimed and blind and lame." The guest list should sound familiar. When Matthew tells this story (22:1-10), he makes the point even stronger, saying that the servant gathered up "both bad and good" to fill the hall.

So, at the table, the table of Jesus, there is shock and surprise. Insiders become outsiders and outsiders become insiders, and we are surprised to find the strangest sort of people there where two or three are gathered. Dutch pastor Nico Ter Linden tells us that they have an expression in Holland which illustrates Matthew's point. Whenever the Dutch come across someone on the street who is obviously not quite together mentally or who is odd or unconven-

tional in his behavior they say, "The dear Lord keeps strange boarders at his table.

The Invitation

For most of us, when we think of the Lord's Supper, this holy meal which you now celebrate as your pastor takes her place behind the table and begins the Prayer of Thanksgiving, we think about the Last Supper which Jesus ate with his disciples in the upper room. It is natural that we should think of this meal which culminated Jesus' earthly ministry. The significance of this meal is not simply in the words which Jesus repeated as he passed the bread and wine, "This is my body. . . . this is my blood," but as with the other meals, the significance is in the talk that takes place around the table and in the presence of the guests. Here is the only meal in which Jesus is the host. He begins, "I shall not eat . . . until it is fulfilled in the kingdom of God" (Luke 22:16). He says that he shall fast until the kingdom comes.

Then, as was Hebrew custom, he takes and blesses the cup of wine, predicting, "I shall not drink of the fruit of the vine until the kingdom of God comes" (22:18). After the cup is blessed, the bread is blessed, broken, and given with the strange words, "This is my body."

After this, Jesus drops the bombshell: "Behold the hand of him who betrays me is with me on the table." All the disciples are uncertain as to who will betray him, for "they began to question one another, which of them it was that would do this." The disciples know enough to know that no one is secure from the temptation to betray Jesus.

As it turns out, their fears are well founded. Next there is a dispute over greatness. After we get him elected Messiah, who will be able to sit with him on his cabinet? they want to know (22:24-27). Here, at the very end of Jesus' ministry, his twelve best friends, those who have been with Jesus throughout his ministry, reveal by their conversation that they have not the slightest understanding of his kingdom. Has he not told them that here the first shall be last and the last first? Jesus is among them this night as always, not as the triumphant Lord but as the "one who serves." He is the waiter, the deacon, the servant. In serving them food and drink he enacts the pattern for ministry. Here Jesus waits on the table as he prepares to go die on a cross, and they argue about greatness. They all reveal, in this argument, that they have not the slightest understanding of his mission. They do betray him.

Later, when Caesar's soldiers come to carry Jesus away, both the disciples and the soldiers have swords. They both participate in the powers of darkness. There is pitifully little difference between them. Satan possesses them both. Judas betrays Jesus with a kiss, the other disciples betray Jesus with their dispute over greatness, their cowardice, and their violence. They all flee into the darkness as Jesus is dragged away.

And yet, behind this dark and sad tale is the reassurance of Jesus who, even as he is being led away to death, says to his disciples that he is going to prepare a place for them at a new banquet table to come (22:28-30). He goes to prepare a place for *them*.

Now, as the invitation to the table is given by your pastor and your church begins to come forward, you begin to see the wonder of it all: Jesus continues to invite half-hearted, misunderstanding, sometimes faithful and sometimes foolish disciples to eat with him. Sinners continue to be his main dinner companions everytime the church eats and drinks with Jesus.

For that grace, experienced so vividly at the table, we can be grateful.

With Glad and Generous Hearts

Of course, if we told only the story of the Last Supper, we wouldn't be telling the whole story about the Lord's Supper. We Christians worship not on Thursday evening but on Sunday morning. We do so because that was the day of Easter, the day of resurrection, the day when we, with the disciples, realized much to our surprise that the Jesus story was beginning rather than ending.

On that first Easter evening, two disciples were walking dejectedly down the road to the little village of Emmaus. A stranger appeared and walked with them (Luke 24:13-35).

"What are you talking about as you walk?" the stranger asks.

Sadly they respond, "Are you the only visitor to Jerusalem who does not know the things that have happened there in these days?"

They then tell the stranger about how they had hoped that Jesus of Nazareth would be "the one to redeem Israel" but that he had been put to death. The disciples, blinded by their despair, failed to recognize the risen Christ. "And beginning with Moses and all the prophets, he interpreted to them in all the scriptures the thing concerning himself" (vs. 27).

Still, they see nothing. When they arrive at Emmaus, the disciples bid the stranger to stay with them. Then, "when he was at table with them, he took the bread and blessed, and broke it, and gave it to them. And their eyes were opened and they recognized him" (vss. 30-31).

Don't you find it interesting that they recognized him only when he was at table with them? They did not see him, even when he interpreted the scriptures for them. It was only when Jesus repeated those familiar four-fold table actions of taking, blessing, breaking, and giving of bread that they were given the recognition. It was only at the table that the scripture made sense, that their eyes were opened and that they at last began to understand what was happening among them. And they ran all the way back to Jerusalem to tell the others "what happened on the road, and how he was known to them in the breaking of the bread" (vs. 35).

Do you feel that way now, as you come forward to the table? Words are not enough. Words were not enough then, when talk was not cheap and even one so great as Jesus was doing the Bible study and preaching, and words are not enough today. Therefore, your church gathers and hears the word read from the Bible, preached from the pulpit, affirmed in the creed; then we offer gifts of bread and wine so that they might be taken for the work of upbuilding God's people, blessed for the holy use of God's holy ones, broken and passed around for everyone who accepts the invitation to come, and given as a tangible, visible assurance that "where two or three are gathered in my name, there am I in the midst of them" (Matt. 18:20).

As it was at Emmaus that first Easter Sunday evening, so it is for your church on this Sunday morning—something happens at the Lord's table that
doesn't happen anywhere else in the church's worship. Did not Jesus promise his disciples, before his
crucifixion, "You may eat and drink at my table in my
kingdom" (Luke 22:30)? That evening at Emmaus,
and at the following meals on the beach, in the room
on pentecost, in the early church's eating and drinking together, the disciples experienced the beginning
of the new age. The promised banquet table of the
Lord is now.

The main requirement to be seated at that table is
the same now as it was then: to be needy, empty, and
hungry. Here we come singing, "Just as I am without
one plea, but that thy blood was shed for me." We
come weak, hungry, despondent. We leave shouting,
with the first disciples, "He is risen!"

This table is our foretaste of the kingdom. Here
Jesus' kingdom begins to take visible form, here we
see the sort of kingdom God intends for the whole
world—sinners are forgiven, the poor are invited,
and the hungry are fed.

There are so many things which the church doesn't
do very well. We, like those first disciples, are often
faithless, misunderstanding, confused, and cow-
ardly. When the going gets rough, we follow them
into the safety of the darkness. Rather than trust the
power of Jesus and his truth, we pick up the sword
and fight Caesar on Caesar's terms. No wonder when
Jesus' little band of followers gathers on Sunday
morning we are apt to be depressed, downcast, despondent, and empty.

Then we offer the bread and wine, along with our

lives; we bless these gifts as signs of God's continual care for us; we give the bread and wine and feast upon this enactment of love. In so doing our eyes are opened. We see that it is not all left up to us in worship or in life. Our actions are but loving responses to the God who, in bread and wine and the everyday stuff of life, has reached out to us. We shall not go away from worship hungry. Rather, we shall leave refreshed, strengthened for the week which lies ahead, renewed by the table fellowship.

Pay attention to yourself and your fellow Christians at the table. Here is the most basic, most universal, most biblical gathering of the body of Christ. Who is the church? That sometimes sinful, sometimes faithful body which gathers on Sunday to hear the word and then enact the word in wine and bread, that group who has been invited and then gifted to celebrate this holy meal "with glad and generous hearts" (Acts 2:46).

9.

Sending Forth
The Lord bless you and keep you.

The Lord bless you and keep you:
The Lord make his face to shine upon you,
   and be gracious to you:
The Lord lift up his countenance upon you,
   and give you peace.

—Numbers 6:24-26

The table is cleared. The pastor puts things back in order. The last hymn is sung, and then she stands before the congregation. All rise. The pastor faces everyone, stretches out her arms, as if in embrace, and says, "The Lord bless you and keep you: The Lord make his face to shine upon you, and be gracious to you: The Lord lift up his countenance upon you, and give you peace. *Amen.*"

"I hate to say goodbye," we sometimes say. "Parting is such sweet sorrow," says Juliet to her Romeo. The end of today's service is an event of worship which is full of threat and promise. The blessing before we go forth is a brief act, the significance of which we might miss if we are not careful.

There is threat in this ending. A couple of hours ago you were at home, alone, contemplating the events that were to come. From your solitude you have been moved to community, the holy together-ness which is at the heart of Christian worship. There is strength in numbers. In raising your voice with others, in blending your journey of faith with those of your fellow pilgrims, you have been summoned from your solitude and you have felt strengthened. Things happen in church, when we are together, that cannot happen anywhere else.

But now, with our departure, comes the real test of our prayer and praise. Will you discover later, when you are far from this assembly, that this time of wor-ship has been only an escape which quickly blurs and fades when exposed to the harsh light of the real world? Will the power ebb and will you feel terribly alone, terribly severed from the source of life when you walk out these doors?

Even as there is threat in this ending, there is also promise. It is the promise that this ending shall be a beginning. You have willingly exposed yourself to the force of God's word, and God's table, and God's people. What difference will that make? You can't say for sure, for the difference will be "out there," in the world, in the way you spend your time, and your money, and your life. In any ending something dies—this service, this moment, your old self. And something may be reborn; that is the promise. So some Sunday you depart enthusiastically (literally "filled with the Spirit"), ready to share what you have received, to tell what you have heard, to do what you have decided.

The blessing, or benediction, is now spoken as a promise that, as you depart, God goes with you.

In the Hebrew scriptures, the act of blessing confers power on a person. A father blesses his son (Gen. 27), people bless one another upon departure (Gen. 47:10). "The Lord is with you" (Judg. 6:12) is the greeting and the farewell which makes life bearable.

In the Bible, worship is always concluded with blessing. Therefore, an important function of priests is to bless people. Israel's priests are those who bless.

> The Lord said to Moses, "Say to Aaron and his sons, Thus you shall bless the people of Israel: you shall say to them,
> > The Lord bless you and keep you:
> > The Lord make his face to shine upon you, and be gracious to you:
> > The Lord lift up his countenance upon you, and give you peace.
> So shall they put my name upon the people of Israel, and I will bless them.
>
> *—Numbers 6:22-27*

To bless people in the name of the God of Israel is to literally lay God's name on them, to "put my name upon the people of Israel" (Num. 6:27).

In everyday life we do not think much about the sacredness of our moments of departure except when we send someone for a long or hazardous journey, or bid farewell to a loved one who is entering serious surgery, or send a child away to college. These sweet, painful moments point us toward the holiness of leave-taking. The French *adieu*, the Spanish *adios*, the

English *goodbye* are all derived from "God be with you." They are all human well-wishings which lay the name of God upon another person.

Parting is such sweet sorrow because, in bidding farewell, how can we know that we shall meet again? How can we predict all that might happen to us in the intervening time? God knows. So we say "God be with you" in recognition that our comings and goings are in the hands of God, not our own, and that the steadfast love of God goes with us.

Blessed to Be a Blessing

Paul speaks of Christ as God's blessing (Gal. 3:8-9,14). Jesus is here to bless us. He blesses children (Mark 10:13-16) and meals (Mark 6:41; 8:6-7). At the Lord's Supper, he blesses the bread and the cup (Mark 14:22-23). He blesses his disciples (Luke 24:50-51). Then he tells them to go out and bless others, even those who may curse them (Luke 6:28). In so doing, Jesus makes blessing a sign of the radical nature of discipleship, for the disciples are to bless even those who may persecute or curse them, even as God sends the blessings of sun and rain upon the just and the unjust, the good and the bad (Matt. 5:44-45).

In writing to the Ephesians Paul shouts, "Blessed be the God and Father of our Lord Jesus Christ, who has blessed us in Christ with every spiritual blessing" (Eph. 1:3).

Blessing is not just for church but is also for the world. The Christian is the one who, in the name of Christ, says to the whole world, even to those who curse us, "The Lord is with you."

As your pastor raises her hands in blessing, you can feel the power, the power of one human being upholding another, the power of one person saying to another, "The Lord is with you." This isn't a prayer to God or a pious human wish. This is a statement of fact.

This fact makes re-entry into the world possible. You don't know what you will encounter tomorrow at work. What headlines will fill Monday's newspaper? What new challenges, higher hurdles, tougher tasks will come your way? You don't know. All you know is, "If God is for us, who is against us?" (Rom. 8:31). All human life, all community, is built upon this foundation.

Christ's disciples are sent forth (Matt. 10, Luke 10) not only with a message of the coming kingdom; they are also sent to bless, to make visible, in word and in deed, that God is with us. In your pastor's act of blessing, all human leave-taking is transformed as an everyday opportunity to commend another person to God. All our social action, good deeds, charity, work for justice are means of blessing the world in God's name, laying upon an unknowing world our knowledge that, "The Lord is with you."

God Be with You

Having been blessed in this time of worship, you go forth, knowing that God goes with you. Be careful. In the bright glare of the sunlit parking lot at midday, on the way down the freeway toward home, while you are at work on Monday, it may be easy to forget that fact. The presence of God, the love and action of God are just as real outside the church as within. But your own awareness of that love and action may not be. So, as you go about your duties next week, remember what has happened to you here. Recall the sights and

the sounds, the stories, the words, the bread and the
wine, the blessing of one with hands outstretched
before you saying, as Jesus said to his first disciples,
"All authority in heaven and on earth has been given
to me. Go therefore and make disciples of all nations
. . . and lo, I am with you always, to the close of the
age" (Matt. 28:18-20).

EDUCATIONAL GUIDE
by John H. Westerhoff III

EDUCATIONAL GUIDE

*W*ith *Glad and Generous Hearts* marks the third of my friend and colleague's books for lay persons, especially those in the United Methodist tradition, on worship. Once again Will Willimon has penned a book that will stimulate conversation, learning, and reform in Christian worship.

In his first book, *Remember Who You Are: Baptism, a Model for Christian Life*, Dr. Willimon established that baptism is the rite of initiation for Christians into a community which celebrates and lives the Eucharist. In his second book, *Sunday Dinner: The Lord's Supper and the Christian Life*, he established that the standard celebration for Christian worship is the weekly celebration of the Eucharist, which moves from the proclamation of the scriptures to participation in the Lord's Supper. Now, in this book, he explores the normative shape of Sunday worship and the meaning of its various parts.

While most of his examples and judgments are especially directed to United Methodists and those of similar traditions, the shape of the liturgy he recommends and its meanings are shared by all Christians and will be familiar to Lutherans, Episcopalians, and Roman Catholics. The study guide which follows, therefore, like the book itself, is focused particularly for United Methodists. Others who choose to use it will need to make adaptations which address their denominations' concerns.

While this book can be profitably read by individuals, it may also be used as a resource for group study and discussion. For education purposes a group of six to ten persons is best. If a church school class or study group of youth or adults has more members, they may wish to work in small groups and share their work at the end of a session.

This educational guide is divided into eight sessions which include suggestions for individual preparation and suggestions for group discussion and activity. I recommend that a group spend a minimum of an hour together each session. The eight sessions are based on the shape of the liturgy affirmed by most all Christians, namely:

Gather in Christ's Name
Proclaim and Respond to the Word of God
Pray for the World and the Church
Exchange the Peace
Prepare the Table, Make Eucharist, Break the Bread, and Share the Gifts of God
Go Forth in the Name of Christ

The intention of these educational sessions is for enlightenment. However, since what Dr. Willimon defends as normative in the church and recommends for weekly worship is not typical in all congregations, it is hoped that this educational guide will provide a resource for the reform of the church's worship.

SESSION ONE

In Preparation:

- Secure copies of a typical Sunday worship service in your congregation.
- Have one or more members of your class or group interview the pastor and/or members of the worship committee. Seek answers to the following questions:

  How long has this service been used?
  When was it last changed?
  What changes were made? Why?
  What is the meaning of the present order?
  Why is it the way it is?

- Read the introduction to *With Glad and Generous Hearts*.

When the Group Gathers:

- Get acquainted and then pass out copies of your typical Sunday worship service. Report on what you learned.
- Put the following outline on newsprint for everyone to see.

        Gathering of the Church
            Greeting
            Hymn
            Opening Prayers
            Confession and Pardon
            Act of Praise

Proclamation and Praise
   Prayer of Illumination
   Scripture Lection (Old Testament)
   Psalm or Anthem
   Scripture Lection (Epistle)
   Hymn
   Gospel Lection
   Sermon
Responses and Offering
   Affirmation of Faith (Creed)
   Concerns and Prayers for Others
   The Peace
   Offering
Holy Meal
   Taking Bread and Cup
   Great Thanksgiving with Lord's Prayer
   Breaking Bread
   Giving Bread and Cup
Sending Forth
   Hymn
   Dismissal with Blessing

- Compare and contrast your Sunday worship with this outline. Ask the following:

   Where is it the same and different? Why?
   What questions do we have about this order?
   What questions do we have about the differences between them?

- Give the members of the group the opportunity to answer these questions. Record those not answered and seek to find the answers during this study.
- Close the first session by asking each person to share memories of, "My favorite Sunday in this church."

SESSION TWO

In Preparation:
- Read chapters 1-3 in *With Glad and Generous Hearts*.
- Consider the following statements:

  1. Without a proper gathering of the church, worship is ineffective.
  2. The sins we confess at worship are the sins of the church, and by confessing those sins we establish the nature and character of the church.
  3. Worship can be escapist and sick or engaging and healthy; it can be solely for the people who attend, or it can be directed toward our relationship with a living, acting God.

- Note below the feelings these statements surfaced in you, the insights you gained through reflecting on them, and the implications you believe they have for worship in your congregation.

When the Group Gathers:

- Encourage each person to share their preparation notes. Accept each person's thoughts and feelings without judgment. Listen carefully so as to better understand one another and your present beliefs and attitudes about worship.
- Have each person complete the following statements:

I go to church because _____.
When I go to church I expect _____.
Sin is _____.
Repentance is _____.
The church is _____.
Worship helps us to _____.

- Share your answers and discuss them. Compare and contrast them with those suggested by Dr. Willimon in the chapters assigned.
- Establish one or more propositions on what it means for a community of faith to gather in the name of Christ.
- Establish ways you believe your Sunday worship needs to be reformed if you are to take seriously these propositions. List these ideas on chalkboard or newsprint.

SESSION THREE

In Preparation:
- Read chapters 4-6 in *With Glad and Generous Hearts*.
- Consider the following statements:

  1. The lessons read and preached about on Sunday at worship should be those assigned in the church's lectionary.
  2. Going to church on Sunday is not primarily to hear an inspiring sermon.
  3. To be a Christian is to believe what the church believes as found in the church's creeds.

- Note below the feelings these statements elicited in you, the insights you gained through reflecting on them, and the implications you believe they have for worship in your congregation.

When the Group Gathers:

- Encourage each person to share his or her preparation notes. Accept each person's thoughts and feelings without judgment. Listen carefully so as to better understand one another.
- Have each person complete the following statements:

    The purpose of reading the scripture at worship is
    _____.

    The purpose of the sermon is _____.
    The purpose of the affirmation of the church's faith
    is _____.

- Share your answers and discuss them. Compare and contrast your answers with those suggested by Dr. Willimon in the chapters assigned.
- On newsprint, list all the characteristics of a "good" sermon.
- On newsprint, list some of the ways you might become a better listener to the scripture and sermon.

SESSION FOUR

In Preparation:
- Read chapter 7 in *With Glad and Generous Hearts*.
- Consider the following statements:

  1. We are to pray for what God wills to do.
  2. The prayers of the people should be led by a lay person and not the pastor.
  3. Prayers for others or intercessions are an essential dimension of Sunday worship.

- Note below the feelings these statements surfaced in you, the insights you gained through reflecting on them, and the implications you believe they have for worship in your congregation.

When the Group Gathers:

- Encourage each person to share his or her preparation notes. Accept each person's thoughts and feelings without judgment. Listen carefully so as to better understand one another.
- Have each person complete the following statements:

    Prayer is _____.
    Praying for the world and the church is important because _____.
    Intercessory prayers make a difference because
    _____.
    The purpose of prayer is _____.

- Share your answers and discuss them. Compare and contrast your answers with those suggested by Dr. Willimon in the chapter assigned.
- Encourage each person to share his or her positive or negative experiences with prayer.
- In what ways does your church "teach us to pray"?

SESSION FIVE

In Preparation:
- Read chapter 8 in *With Glad and Generous Hearts*.
- Note how you feel, on a scale from one to five, when (1) the Peace is shared in Sunday worship, (2) the Offering is received.

	Unmeaningful			*Meaningful*	
The Peace	1	2	3	4	5
The Offering	1	2	3	4	5

- Think about some of the reasons why you feel this way about these activities. Be prepared to share your feelings with the group.
- Consider the following statements:

  1. We are more apt to act our way into a new way of thinking than we are to think our way into a new way of acting.

  2. In the church there are to be no strangers or estranged people.

  3. The Peace is not a time to get acquainted.

  4. Acting out the Peace is essential to coming to the Lord's table.

  5. Christian worship is a material affair.

  6. The way we use our money is a good indicator of our values.

- Note below the feelings these statements surfaced in you, the insights you gained through reflecting on them, and the implications you believe they have for worship in your congregation.

When the Group Gathers:

- Encourage each person to share their preparation notes. Accept each person's thoughts and feelings without judgment. Listen carefully so as to better understand one another.
- Have each person complete the following statements:

> To exchange the Peace is _____.
> The Peace is for me _____.
> The Peace is in our church _____.
> The Peace in our congregation needs _____.
> The Offering would be more meaningful if we
> _____.

- Share your answers and discuss them.
- Establish one or more propositions on what it means to exchange the Peace and to offer ourselves and our gifts to God.
- Establish specific ways you believe your Sunday worship needs to be reformed if you are to take seriously these propositions.

SESSION SIX

In Preparation:
- Read or review chapter 8 in *With Glad and Generous Hearts*.
- Assign one or more persons to read Will Willimon's book *Sunday Dinner*. Have this person or these persons prepare to report to the group on this book.
- Consider the following statements:

  1. The Lord's Supper needs to be celebrated every Sunday.
  2. The Offering is the bridge that yokes what we say with what we do.
  3. The experience of the living Christ is most fully experienced in the breaking of the bread and the drinking of the cup at the Lord's table.

- Note below the feelings these statements surfaced in you, the insights you gained through reflecting on them, and the implications you believe they have for worship in your congregation.

166

- The Lord's Supper is full of symbols and symbolic gestures. What visual symbol comes to your mind as you ponder the significance of this sacrament? Draw that symbol in the space below.

When the Group Gathers:

- Encourage each person to share their preparation notes. Accept each person's thoughts and feelings without judgment. Listen carefully so as to better understand one another.
- Have the persons who read *Sunday Dinner* share their report with the group.
- Establish one or more propositions on what it means to participate in the sacrament of the Lord's Supper.
- Establish ways you believe your Sunday worship needs to be reformed if you are to take seriously these propositions.
- Share your visual symbols of the Lord's Supper. Compare and discuss them together.

SESSION SEVEN

In Preparation:
- Read chapter 9 in *With Glad and Generous Hearts.*
- Consider the following statements:

    1. Those who participate in worship should live lives that have identifiable characteristics.
    2. Worship is the primary responsibility of the church; everything else it does is secondary.
    3. The vitality of the church is measured by the lives lived during the week of those who worship on Sunday.

- Note below the feelings these statements surfaced in you, the insights you gained through reflecting on them, and the implications you believe they have for worship in your congregation.

- **Thinking back on your life, when were you blessed by someone at some significant moment of leave taking?**

When the Group Gathers:

- Encourage each person to share their preparation notes. Accept each person's thoughts and feelings without judgment. Listen carefully so as to better understand one another.
- Have each person complete the following statements:

  To participate in worship should make a difference in _____.
  Leaving church after worship should _____.
  To be blessed is _____.
  We go forth to _____.

- Establish one or more propositions on what it means to go forth in the name of Christ.
- Establish ways you believe your Sunday worship needs to be reformed if you are to take seriously these propositions.
- Share your memories of significant "blessings" at leave taking. How do these memories enrich and inform your experience of the blessing on Sunday morning?

SESSION EIGHT

In Preparation:

- Answer the following questions:

    1. What did you experience during these seven weeks?

    2. How do you feel about this experience?

    3. What insights did you gain?

    4. What implications does your learning have for your life?

- Ask your pastor to come to the final session and be prepared to preside at the Word and Table service discussed in the first meeting.

When the Group Gathers:

- Imagine that you are trying to respond to the question of your six-year-old child, "Why do I have to go to church on Sunday morning?" Take turns sharing what you might say to your child.

- Review the implications you arrived at in each of your previous sessions.

- Reflect on these and make recommendations to the pastor, the worship committee, and official board for the reform of worship in your congregation.

- Celebrate the Lord's Supper.

Scripture Index

Old Testament

Subject Index

About the Author

William Willimon is Minister to the University and Professor of the Practice of Christian Ministry at Duke University in Durham, North Carolina. He received the M.Div. degree from Yale Divinity School and the S.T.D. degree from Emory University. Dr. Willimon has served several United Methodist churches in Georgia and South Carolina.

Among his many published works are *Remember Who You Are: Baptism, a Model for Christian Life* and *Sunday Dinner: The Lord's Supper and the Christian Life.*

Dr. Willimon and his wife Patricia have two children, William Parker and Harriet Patricia.